The RFD News

Chuck Cecil

Library of Congress Control Number: 2003095559

ISBN: 1-893490-05-X

Printed in the United States of America
PINE HILL PRESS
4000 West 57th Street
Sioux Falls, S.D. 57106

Table of Contents

Out on the Rural Routes

An Introduction

Several years ago I edited and published a supplement that was inserted into our weekly newspapers. It contained pictures, news, and feature items gathered mostly from the rural routes which we felt would be of interest to rural residents. We called the supplement *The RFD News,* and the business name we gave to our little family of nine weekly newspapers was registered as The RFD News Group, Inc.

A question often asked, particularly by younger readers, was what the initials RFD in the newspaper's name stood for. Some thought that it was honoring a former president, Franklin Delano Roosevelt. But that was FDR, not RFD. Others through it stood for Rural Federal Delivery, but that wasn't it, either.

RFD is the Postal Service abbreviation of "Rural Free Delivery." Rather than write out this long address as, for example, "Rural Free Delivery Route Two, Box 73," the farm families took the shorter, easier way, simply jotting down "RFD." The plan originally was to deliver mail free of charge to rural families. It had a tremendous impact, especially in less populated, more rural states like South Dakota. Until Rural Free Delivery, farm family mail was picked up at the post offices in nearby towns, and a trip to town, at best, was usually a once-a-week endeavor. The plan of weekday mail delivery to the farm driveway would not have the impact of rural electrification or the remarkable mechanization of farm equipment, of course, but RFD did change life out on the farm, and aided in the growth and development of agriculture. As important, it also had an impact on farm family life and the farming community's close-knit social structure.

In the early, formative days of Rural Free Delivery, all sorts of items arrived at the end of the farm driveway. It might be letters or postcards, newspapers, catalogs, and even packages, including ungainly cardboard boxes with small circular openings cut out on the sides that contained a noisy batch of baby chicks. This outside contact helped smooth the rough, rural edges and reduce the mental depression and loneliness brought on particularly to the women left home alone in tiny huts on isolated farmsteads where there was nothing much to make even a shadow. RFD brought people closer together and brought to their homes information to educate and encourage the use of new farming methods and technologies.

Rural Free Delivery began as an experiment in West Virginia in 1918. The farm families on the routes selected were delighted with the new service and with the new world brought to them each weekday. After receiving free mail delivery for a few months, one farmer observed that it would take away part of life to give it up.

Another farmer from Missouri, when rural routes reached that state, looked back on his life before RFD and calculated that in the fifteen years before Rural Free Delivery, he had traveled twelve thousand miles going to and from the post office in the nearby town to pick up his mail.

A serendipitous result of Rural Free Delivery was the stimulation it provided to the development of the unmatched American system of roads and highways. A prerequisite for rural delivery in the early days was the availability of good roads for the rural mail carrier to use. After hundreds of petitions for rural delivery were turned down by the Post Office because of inaccessible, impassable roads which literally evolved from wagon ruts, responsible local governments were pressured by rural families and neighborhoods and compelled to extend and improve existing highways.

Between 1897 and 1908, these local governments spent an estimated $72 million on bridges, culverts, and other road improvements. In one county in Indiana, farmers themselves paid over $2,600 to grade and gravel a road in order to qualify for Rural Free Delivery. Often, rural families volunteered part of a working day to join neighbors in improving the rural roads in their vicinity to insure the uninterrupted delivery of mail and commerce. The improvements on our highways and byways stimulated the growth in the sale of automobiles. In his book *America*, English author Alistair Cooke wrote that Henry Ford's Model T car "gave farmers miles away from anywhere a new pair of legs." So, too, did the decision to provide free mail delivery to rural families, who looked forward each year to receiving in their rural mailboxes the weekly issue of their newspapers and their new copies of what became known as "Wish Books," which were the Sears Roebuck and Montgomery-Ward catalogs.

The impact of RFD as a cultural and social agent for millions of Americans was even more striking, and in this respect rural delivery is still an important link between industrial and rural America.

The establishment of rural delivery was a heady taste of life for rural Americans, and they soon increased their demand for delivery of small packages, such as foodstuffs, tobacco, dry goods, and commodities not easily available to farmers.

With the recent national changes to street and avenue addresses for rural families, initiated primarily to aid law enforcement and emergency response teams in finding specific farmsteads, the days of the RFD route are ending. Rural route addresses are being replaced by six- and eight-digit home addresses and street and avenue addresses. Those streets and avenues extend across entire states and jump state borders.

This book, *The RFD News*, is a collection of stories about people and places I visited and wrote about over the years as I traveled South Dakota's RFD routes in my capacity as a newspaper reporter, editor, and later publisher. For decades, a hobby of mine has been to collect and to jot down the hum-drum and important but perhaps little-known events and dates of South Dakota happenings from the ridiculous to the sublime.

So along with the regular chapters in *The RFD News*, there are twelve postcard sections that contain news briefs, some of which are of great historic significance for South Dakota and some that in the grand scheme of things probably are of no importance whatsoever. These small, inconsequential snapshots are in many respects very similar to the brief messages hurriedly written on picture postcards, which were the most common medium for communication between friends and families in the early days, mailed for a penny back to the home place in South Dakota, out along the Rural Free Delivery routes.

Dear Mom and Dad:

  Saw Abe Lincoln's cabin birthplace at fair today. It wa leaning a bit, and looked small for such a big man. Ha.

  Be home Saturday. Take care

George B
P.S.—Say hello to sis for me.

POST CARD

Mr. and Mrs. Ted Burgen
RFD 4, Box 33
El

LINCOLN'S BIRTHPLACE
CHICAGO WORLD'S FAIR - 1933

Chapter 1

Barn Straightener

You won't find barn straighteners listed in the yellow pages. Barn
straighteners don't hand out business cards or set up booths at
winter farm shows.

In fact, you won't find very
many barn straighteners anywhere,
anymore. More and more old barns
along the old RFD routes are being
brought to their knees, their raddled
timbers and siding mixed like a
giant's game of Pick-Up-Sticks, then
burned on chilly fall days to make
room for the tin box pole barns that

Midwestern barn straightener Ray
Chamberlain of rural Sinai. *Chuck Cecil
Photo*

seem to be the rage in these days of tight budgets and instant gratifica-
tion. The independent barn straighteners of America are a disappearing
breed.

But Ray Chamberlain of Sinai is hanging in there. His mission in life
is to put old barns straight with the world again.

Ray, in his early 70s, is one of the last of the masters in the barn
straightening business. He has more barns on his "a-kilter list" than he
knows what to do with. Prairie winds, a tornado now and then, and the
propensity for wood to gradually rot away and seek sea level keeps him
very busy.

His straightened prairie monuments stand tall again from
Minneapolis to the Nebraska Sand Hills. Most of his work is in South
Dakota. But he'll go anywhere he's needed. "I like the challenge," he
said. "And I haven't found a barn yet that I couldn't fix."

At one time, his seven sons chipped in, helping him tighten the
wind-humming cables, rig up heavy timber braces, and work the greasy
jacks possessing Herculean lifting powers. Back then, Chamberlain's
little notebook tucked over his heart in the wide pocket between the
suspenders of his bib overalls had sixty or seventy barns on his waiting
list. But now the boys have long-since grown and are busy elsewhere.
Chamberlain has for several years carried the load himself. But he

admits that as he grows older, his barn straightening muscles are scanning the prairie horizon looking for a rocking chair on a shady front porch. He's slowing down.

"I need a farm boy to help me," he said, flipping his red-checkered cap forward to scratch an itch on his barn-dust-encrusted scalp. "A city boy couldn't stand up to all this hard work."

Chamberlain figures he's brought about four thousand barns back to plumb in the over thiry-five years he's been at it. During that time, he's discovered the hard way that straightening old barns can be dangerous. "I've had eight broken ribs and two skull fractures when things didn't go just the way I'd planned them," he said.

He grew up on a ranch near White River, SD, raised around skittish cattle and mean-spirited horses that were expert and adept at pawing, kicking, and biting. "There was always a kicked-in corral to fix, so I learned about bracing and using big timber as a boy," he said. Later, he taught school in White River, then worked as a carpenter in the Dupree area. After that he managed a Waubay lumberyard, where he learned even more about the strengths and weaknesses of wood and where and how to drive the spikes and nails to insure the strongest bond.

Chamberlain's barn-straightening career began one day after a vicious storm dropped down on the Waubay area and damaged many farm buildings. A local insurance adjuster asked Chamberlain's wife Blanche if she knew anyone who could straighten a leaning barn. She volunteered Ray.

Virgil Strenge with his storm-damaged barn and its perilous lean to the east, before being pulled back to plumb by expert barn straightener Ray Chamberlain. *Chuck Cecil Photo*

"Heck, I'd never done anything like that before," Chamberlain said, "but she told him I could fix anything." He accepted the straightening job and learned from his mistakes. But he also learned how to counteract the forces of gravity, and he bought some valuable old barn straightening equipment from a barn straightener who was clearing out his tool shed and heading for retirement. Since then, Ray's inventive mind has also crafted other helpful barn straightening tools.

"I've always been kind of a tinkerer and I liked to figure out how to solve problems," he said, "so I've found this business to be a lot of fun."

A few years ago he was working at the Virgil Strenge farm south of Brookings, cranking away on a stubborn old barn nearly falling in on itself. A tornado had ripped through the Strenge farmstead in the dead of a spring night and slammed full-force into the open door of the old barn that had been a part of Strenge's life since childhood. Strenge's house was also damaged, but the barn took the brunt of the force. It was bent and blown off its foundation a half-foot or so. The tornado forced its way out the east end opposite the big barn door on the west side. It was a mess, and Strenge thought the tornado's blow was probably fatal to his old, familiar friend.

He hated the thought of losing that old barn. "My granddad built it in 1919. I played in it as a boy and worked in it as a man. When I was in grade school, the barn was my first sighting of home I saw after school was out. One of my boys and I had planned to fix it up someday just for old time's sake," Strenge said.

Ray Chamberlain prepares to ratchet the south side of Virgil Strenge's barn back into plumb using levers, pulleys, and cables of his own design. *Chuck Cecil Photo*

But the barn's condition after the tornado seemed critical. "I figured I'd have to tear it down before it fell down," he said. As a next to last resort, he called Chamberlain.

The Sinai barn straightener drove over and inspected the damage. It would present Chamberlain "the tinkerer" with a little more figuring than he was accustomed to. For starters, the barn's loft was nearly filled with about eighty thousand pounds of baled hay. It presented the kind of challenge Chamberlain enjoyed solving.

He accepted the job, provided Strenge was available when a little more horse power was needed for some of the tricky work of barn straightening. On the day work was to commence, Chamberlain arrived at the Strenge farm with his trusty old service truck packed with common and uncommon barn straightening accoutrements.

There were six hundred or seven hundred feet of half-inch cable, various and sundry pulleys, ladders of every length, and a collection of railroad ties and heavy timber. He uses hand winches that can be coaxed into applying about seventy thousand pounds of barn pulling power. He attached cables in just the right places, and after the preliminaries were in place, Chamberlain levered the sagging Strenge barn, hay bales and all, back into plumb. He then pulled it back on its original foundation, inch by creaking inch, nailed support timbers across the wall studs, and scrambled up and down ladders to patch up the blown-out siding on the barn's east end.

Although the tornado-damaged end of the barn still needs repair, the result of Chamberlain's efforts can be seen in this picture of the straightened barn on the Virgil Strenge farm southwest of Brookings. *Chuck Cecil Photo*

"It's just amazing how he could bring it back," Strenge said after the job was completed. He and his son have since improved the cupola and other parts of the barn so that, unless another tornado comes along, it should be part of the farmstead for years to come.

After the Strenge barn was well again, Chamberlain packed his trusty truck and headed for another job. But he's the first to admit that he's slowing down. "I'm just getting too old for this," he said, climbing down gingerly from a high ladder. When he retires, an era along South Dakota's rural routes will end, too. And old, picturesque barns along our country roads will be the worse for it.

POST CARD

Place the Stamp here
ONE CENT
for United States
Possessions
Canada and
Mexico
CENTS
Foreign

Sophia and Carleen,

Enjoying our visit with grandma and grandpa. Worked all day today and then had to clean house tonight. Be glad to get back home. Write soon.

Love.... Judith

P S - we made brooms from the straw

Sophia Jasperson
Rural Route 5

WHEAT TWO MILES WEST OF ELKTON S.D. 1911   ERICKS FARM

Chapter 2

Master Broom Maker

If there was a sweepstakes award for the world's best broom maker, Edward Tschetter, 57, of Pleasant Valley Hutterite Colony east of Flandreau would surely be among the finalists.

He's a master craftsman at broom making, and he takes pride in every broom he makes.

"I'll put my brooms up against any broom made anywhere," says the colony's personable broom man. He turns out brooms from the colony shop in less time than it takes to sweep most kitchen floors.

Campbell Supply of Sioux Falls has been buying Pleasant Valley's brooms for years. They've become a popular item for house cleaners who are particular about their brooms.

"People ask for corn brooms, and there aren't any that we've found that are better than the Pleasant Valley Colony's brooms," says Carolyn Petersen, a buyer for Campbell Supply.

Edward Tschetter, master broom maker at the Pleasant Valley Hutterite Colony east of Flandreau, poses with some of his finished, hand-made brooms. *Chuck Cecil Photo*

Tschetter, who started as an apprentice in the broom shop as a youngster, figures that only about seven of the state's approximately fifty Hutterite colonies still have broom making shops.

He does most of his broom making in the winter because he's also in charge of the colony's twenty-acre vegetable garden in the spring and summer. In the fall he helps with the butchering as the colony stocks up on meat for the winter.

He's proud of his productive gardens and his expert butchering abilities, but he takes particular pride in the brooms he makes. He does most of the work himself, but as is the custom at the colony, he also has a few colony boys who apprentice in the shop, learning the trade so that one day, they can take his place. The colony's retired broom maker who taught Tschetter is also free to come to the broom room and help if he desires.

The youngsters do most of the hum-drum work in the broom making shop. Until they are older and trained in handling the machinery, they won't be allowed to work with the cutting machines or with the machines that wrap wire around broom handles or stitch the broom straw into place.

The boys eventually graduate to hand-stitching whisk brooms, but most of their after-school work includes attaching the Pleasant Valley Colony label to the brooms, applying price tags, and keeping the shop swept and clean. "The girls work in the home," Tschetter explained. "Just the boys work away from the home after school." Every boy has an assignment helping with some aspect of the colony's work, from watching over turkeys to feeding cattle or working with the crew grinding grain.

Tschetter learned the broom trade as a boy working after school under the tutelage of the colony's now retired broom maker, who taught Tschetter the six steps to making a broom.

There is no assembly line for making the brooms. The Pleasant Valley Colony brooms are made one at a time by one man, who considers the broom on which he is working the most important broom of his life.

First, the broom corn is soaked in a weak dye solution. This softens the corn and gives the stalks a slightly greenish color you'll notice as

Tschetter applies clumps of broom straw to the broom handle which is being spun by this machine. Wire is also being wound around the straw and the handle in this operation. *Chuck Cecil Photo*

the color of choice on store-bought brooms. If the corn isn't softened properly, Tschetter noted, it breaks easily when it is subjected to the second step, which is to wire the corn to the broom handle.

A special machine twirls the broom's handle and wraps wire tightly over five different layers of broom corn, Tschetter explained. Next, the ends of the attached broom corn are combed to remove weak corn stems or stems that did not become attached to the handle during the wire winding.

Tschetter uses a special machine to squeeze the broom straw from a circular arrangement into a broom shape. The machine also stitches the straws into place. *Chuck Cecil Photo*

At this point in the construction, the broom stems are gathered in a circle around the broom handle. Stitching the stems gives the broom a flat, rather than round, bunch of broom straw. The sweeping ends of the corn stems are then trimmed. The final step is to attach the Pleasant Valley Colony label to the broom handle and store it away for sale, use, or shipment.

Tschetter and his eager young apprentices make several different types of brooms. There is the ever-popular household variety, of course, and the colony also makes a more sturdy, industrial broom, a small whisk broom, and a miniature, toy broom. Some of the brooms are used in the colony's sixty-five or so households and some of the industrial brooms help clean out colony pens, sheds, and granaries.

To keep up with the demand, Tschetter makes about 1,500 brooms a year.

At one time, the colony grew its own broom corn for its brooms, but now it buys the straw from Mexico at less cost than if they grew the corn themselves. For the industrial brooms, thicker, sturdier bristles purchased from India are mixed in with the Mexican broom corn.

Tschetter explains that with proper care, his Pleasant Valley Colony broom will last fifteen years or more. And what is proper broom care?

Tschetter said that the common mistake people make with brooms is to store them with the sweeping end up. They should always be hung up off the floor, not set on the floor, and the bristles should always be down so that any moisture can drain out. "If you do that," Tschetter says, "these Pleasant Valley Colony brooms will last a long, long time."

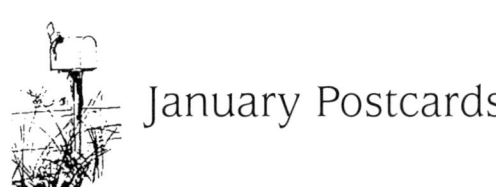 January Postcards

Jan. 1, 1863: At five minutes past midnight, Mahlon Gore, 26, made history by becoming the first homesteader in Dakota Territory, filing for one-quarter section of Sioux River bottom land in Richland Township, Union County, SD. Gore died in 1916.

Jan. 1, 1883: Charles (Badger) Clark, who in 1939 would become South Dakota's poet laureate, was born today in Albia, IA.

Jan. 2, 1884: Oscar Micheaux, who would homestead near Burke before leaving to become a successful black writer and movie producer, was born today in Metropolis, IL. Micheaux made forty-four movies and was considered a motion picture genius. He died in 1951.

Jan. 2, 1935: Edwin and Melvin Walter, ages 11 and 6, left their farm home to visit neighbors who farmed nearby. A blizzard was starting to blow, but they thought they could make the one-mile hike across an open field. They failed to return home for supper that evening and a search was started. They were found early the next morning in a nearby field, huddled together, face down and frozen to death. Their hands were covering their faces, and it was observed that the older boy had apparently removed his coat and placed it over his younger brother's body.

Jan. 2, 1951: Sigurd Anderson of Webster left his law practice today to begin his four-year term as the state's nineteenth governor. He was born Jan. 22, 1904, in Arendel, Norway. He was the last foreign-born South Dakotan to serve as the state's chief executive.

Jan. 3, 1889: It was announced today that Jacob Jenter had discovered a seven-foot deep vein of coal twenty-eight feet below his corn field near Centerville.

Jan. 4, 1866: Niels Hansen, famous horticulturalist at South Dakota State University from 1895 to 1937, was born today in Ribe, Denmark. He would introduce alfalfa and hundreds of other plants and trees to South Dakota during his illustrious career at SDSU.

Jan. 4, 1894: Chief Two Sticks was hanged for murder in Deadwood, Dakota Territory.

Jan. 4, 1962: Don Hight, White River rancher, with help from some of his neighbors, started a 1,800-head cattle drive to the Winner Sale Barn seventy miles away today. The drive, part of it in a raging blizzard with a minus eighty-seven degree wind chill, captured the imagination of the world. Hight received a $353,549 check from the Sale Barn for his cattle.

Jan. 4, 1925: Mr. and Mrs. Claude Emley, rural Martin, started by car for town from their ranch today, but became lost in a sudden storm. They decided to return to their home, but wandered over the prairie in their car for three hours before nearly running into their ranch home in the blinding snow storm.

Jan. 5, 1906: Joe Mendel, one of South Dakota's greatest athletes, was born today on a farm four miles west of Dalton. In 1926, competing for Onida High School, he placed first in four events and won the state track meet single handedly with twenty points. Sioux Falls High School placed second with nineteen, and Miller and Aberdeen tied for third with thirteen points.

Jan. 5, 1971: Elkton native Richard Francis Kniep, who was born Jan.7, 1933, and later became a dairy equipment salesman in Salem, was sworn in as the state's twenty-fifth chief executive today. He served until June 1978, when he was appointed ambassador to Singapore. Lt. Gov. Harvey Wollman of Hitchcock then assumed the governorship.

Gov. Richard Kneip

Jan. 6, 1893: Deecart Hammit of Spencer was born today. He became a banker in Alcester, but is best known as the writer of the song "Hail South Dakota," which in 1943 was named by the Legislature as the official state song. His was one of 158 entries from seventy-six South Dakota communities.

Jan. 6, 1969: Joe Foss, a Sioux Falls businessman and WW II Marine fighter ace who shot down twenty-six Japanese planes, began his four-year term as the twentieth governor today. Foss died at age 88 in Scottsdale, AZ, on Jan. 1, 2003, and was buried at Arlington National Cemetery.

Jan. 7, 1885: The small town of Holabird was organized today and named after a girlfriend of one of the railroaders working on the line passing through town.

Jan. 7, 1960: James Cash Penney visited Mitchell today to dedicate a new J. C. Penney store opening there.

Jan. 8, 1857: Mary Houston Atkinson, the first white child in Dakota Territory, was born today at Ft. Pierre. Later she became mother superior of the Sacred Heart Convent in Chicago. It is said that for weeks after she was born, Indians rode for a considerable distance in the hopes of seeing the new white baby.

Jan. 8, 1927: The promotional train dubbed "The Alfalfa and Sweet Clover Special" began a three thousand-mile journey through seventy-six towns in eastern South Dakota. Nearly fifty thousand people toured the rail car exhibit organized by South Dakota State University to promote the growing of alfalfa and other hardy legumes.

Jan. 9, 1903: President Teddy Roosevelt signed the bill today creating the Wind Cave National Bank in the Black Hills.

Jan. 9, 1895: It became evident today that W. W. Taylor, South Dakota treasurer, had books of state accounts that showed the state treasury was short by about $367,000. He and the cash ended up in South America. The first territorial governor, Arthur Mellette, decided to make up the loss from his own personal estate.

Jan. 9, 1935: Seven children died today in the crash of a Piedmont school bus.

Jan. 10, 1935: The City Marshal of Freeman today asked residents to refrain from dumping ashes from their stoves into the alleys and streets because of nails in the ashes, causing a rash of flat tires in town.

Jan. 10, 1935: The Campbell County Commission voted today to pay wolf bounties and to reward individuals for killing crows, pocket gophers, and magpies. Wolf or coyote bounties were $2 and pups, $1 each. A bounty of ten cents was placed on each gopher, and proof of crows or magpies resulted in payments of five cents each.

Jan. 11, 1904: Sheep rancher William Kunnecke of the Midland area pled guilty today in Ft. Pierre of the brutal murder of Andy Danlers. He was sentenced to life in prison. It was believed that Kunnecke had also killed five other sheepherders who worked for him. Officials believe he killed and buried them rather than pay them for their services. Kunnecke would later escape from the Sioux Falls Penitentiary by hiding in a barrel of discarded cabbage leaves being hauled away from the prison. He was never captured.

Jan. 12, 1988: George and Jennie Crane of near Winfred in Lake County welcomed a new daughter into their home during the blizzard of 1888. She was named Cleo Tempest Crane as a remembrance of the storm.

Jan. 12, 1988: F. J. Feller of rural Groton put his new buggy in a shed as a blizzard passed through the area. Shortly after the storm had ended, his buggy horse walked up on a large snow drift over the shed and fell through, landing on the new buggy, leaving it badly damaged.

Jan. 12, 1936: A bird that Alice Branum of Burke claimed was the world's oldest canary died today. The bird's age is not known. The heart-broken owner died six months later, on July 13th.

Jan. 12, 1888: Mr. Tisland of Oslo Township in Brookings County went out to his well forty rods from his house during the Blizzard of Death which struck today. He became disoriented in the driving snow and was later found frozen to death.

Jan. 12, 1888: A few miles from Tripp in Hutchinson County, rescue workers today found the bodies of nine children and their teacher, Mrs. Anna Wilson, huddled together, frozen to death among the stubble in a corn field. The children and teacher had joined hands when they left the snowbound school house and tried to reach the nearest farm home during the blizzard, which took the lives of 112 South Dakotans.

Jan. 13, 1931: The Schense quadruplets were born today near Hecla.

Jan. 13, 1978: Hubert Humphrey, Wallace native, former high school forensics champion, and mayor of Minneapolis who became a respected U.S. Senator and later Vice President of the U.S., died today of cancer. He was 72.

Wallace native Hubert Humphrey

Jan. 13, 1888: Temperatures hit minus fifty-two degrees in Canistota today.

Jan. 13, 1949: The blizzard of 1949 isolated South Dakota, hitting the West River with such strength that cattle by the thousands died in huge snowdrifts from cold and lack of food. Billy Miner, 17, who went home to his family ranch near Hermosa from Rapid City High School during the Christmas vacation, became ill during the storm. His parents were unable to get medical help due to the closed roads. Before help arrived, the promising athlete died from a ruptured appendix. The three-day blizzard dumped thirty-six inches of snow on level ground and strong winds piled snow drifts as high as houses in the Rapid City area.

Jan. 13, 1877: The first prize fight ever in Deadwood today ended in a fifty-two-round draw.

Jan. 15: 1943: A Chinook wind, which is a fast-moving warm wind, destroyed countless trees in the Black Hills today and gave residents a respite from the cold winter weather. In Spearfish, the temperature at 7:30 a.m. was minus four degrees. Two minutes later, at 7:32, it was forty-nine degrees above zero.

Jan. 15, 1943: WW II ace Joe Foss of Sioux Falls downed his twenty-sixth Japanese plane in the South Pacific today.

Jan. 16, 1932: The first airmail was delivered to Sioux Falls today.

Jan. 17, 1895: A rail car of caged live jackrabbits caught the attention of folks in Winthrop, MN, today. The rabbits had been captured near Willow Lake and were being shipped to England, ordered by several wealthy Brits who hoped to breed them for the popular chase in which fox are usually used.

Jan. 16, 1890: The first ever Inaugural Ball and Governor's Reception in Pierre was held at the newly constructed Locke Hotel.

Jan. 17, 1932: Buckskin Johnny, famous Black Hills character, died today in Butte County.

Jan. 18, 1971: Sen. George McGovern today announced his intention to be a candidate for president.

Jan. 19, 1988: The last five tons of coal were consumed today as a blizzard continued to howl through Flandreau and Moody County. Fears were abated when a train arrived this same evening pulling, among other things, three carloads of hard coal.

Jan. 20, 1937: Movie star Dorothy Provine was born today in Deadwood.

Former Sen. George McGovern

Jan. 20, 1980: A DC-7 with an unusual and illegal cargo landed in a stubble field near Akaska today. To avoid radar detection, it had flown low up the Mississippi and Missouri River valleys, loaded with 25,000 pounds of Columbian marijuana having a street value of $18 million. The landing was scheduled to be made at night, but tailwinds disrupted the plan and the aircraft arrived early. Fishermen out on the ice of the Missouri River watched the landing that Super Bowl Sunday. Assuming the plane was in trouble and making an emergency landing, they went to investigate. They became suspicious, called for help, and parked their pickup trucks in front of the plane so that it could not take off again. The occupants of the aircraft and others involved on the ground preparing battery-powered landing field lights were arrested.

Jan. 21, 1876: Today was the deadline for all Sioux Indians to report to a Dakota Territory agency or be declared hostile.

Jan. 21, 1910: In a speech today in Sturgis, Carrie Nation continued her nationwide efforts to ban liquor sales. She was also escorted to Ft. Meade to speak to horsemen stationed there. Her escorts while in town and at the fort during her visit, unknown to her, were two of the most notorious saloon keepers in Sturgis.

Jan. 22, 1924: State Historian Doane Robinson, who came up with the idea of carving the faces on Mt. Rushmore, first mentioned his "wild idea" at a meeting he was attending in Huron today.

Jan. 23, 1899: Sioux Falls hosted the National Butter Makers Convention today.

Jan. 26, 1900: A group of nineteen beekeepers today formed the South Dakota Beekeepers Association.

Jan. 29, 1902: George B. German, early radio WNAX cowboy singer known for his rendition of "Strawberry Roan" and other western songs, was born today in Princeville, Il.

Jan. 29, 1990: Famous rodeo cowboy Casey Tibbs died today of bone cancer at his home in Ramona, CA. He was one of rodeo's best and most colorful characters. He is buried in the Scotty Philip Cemetery north of Ft. Pierre. On his gravestone, he directed that the following salute to himself and to rodeo horses be engraved: "Thanks for making me look so good. Hell, I was good."

Jan. 30, 1888: Kimball-bound teacher Addie Allen of Boone, IA, died of complications today after a harrowing stage coach ride to her teaching assignment. The stage coach in which she was the lone passenger stalled five miles from town during a blizzard. After spending twenty-two hours huddled in the coach, she and stage driver Charles Gingerly were found and brought to the Kimball House. Gingerly survived, but Miss Allen died after both her frozen feet and arms were amputated in an attempt to save her.

Jan. 30, 1936: Samuel Anderson, a Civilian Conservation Corps (CCC) enrollee serving in the Black Hills, was named today as one of thirty-one All-American CCC baseball players nationally. He was batting .521.

TUCK'S POST CARD

CARTE POSTALE. POSTKARTE.

(FOR ADDRESS ONLY.)

MA and PA

Having wonderful time
wish you were here.
Toured farm science building today and got lost.
Watched milk being puri-
fied. What next?
Sam and Elda

The Ray Ritters House
Volga Post Office

AGRICULTURAL BUILDING
CHICAGO WORLD'S FAIR
1933

Chapter Three

Onion-flavored Milk

I think it was Ben Franklin who said that onions were proof that God loves us and wants us to be happy.

Or maybe he was talking about beer.

Whatever.

The onion crop in these parts pokes out and ripens in the early spring. Big, juicy, hot onions burst out just waiting for the onion lovers among us to mosey up and harvest them.

If you don't like onions, you are not living a full life, and you have absolutely no concept of what rejection is really like.

But I'll take rejection any day over a diet without onions for breakfast, lunch, and dinner. Well, maybe just for lunch and dinner. Can you imagine a hamburger without onions? Or a State Fair midway without the pleasant aroma of onion rings?

I grew up eating onions by the sack full. I learned to eat onions from my mother, who was an avid onion lover. If she felt the urge, she'd whip up an onion sandwich for an afternoon snack and maybe garnish it with thick slices of bitter white radishes. Onions are in my genes. And fortunately, I grew up where onions grew wild in great abundance.

In the 1930s, they sprouted from the iron-hard dirt that was the upper layer of sod on the Wessington Hills, above the little town of Wessington Springs where I was born. Onions grew in profusion up there on those little pint-sized hills, which we called pony hills because of their diminutive size compared to most hills. Up there, we spent glorious summer days on top of our world, dreaming of becoming cowboys out on the Wyoming range or seeing a picture show in the nearby metropolis of Madison out there on the horizon past Woonsocket somewhere.

We pulled those slender green onion tops up, and at the other end was a white, inviting, aromatic onion. We wiped the bulbs on our trouser legs to clear off the clumps of clinging dirt, then munched on them as we hiked the hills and explored the land around tiny Velverndale Lake, searching for the Lost Dutchman Mine and old cavalry forts and remnants of an old, abandoned Indian village. Velverndale, we would learn, was named after the three young children, Vel, Vern and Dale, who had drowned there sometime in the past.

I learned to love those hills and the onions they gave me. I must have had unabated onion breath, but I didn't care. As my mother used to say: "Onion breath is better than no breath at all."

Let's see now, was it Ben Franklin, Lord Halifax, or Floyd the barber who said: "He that leaveth nothing to chance and never eateth an onion will do few things that even resemble excitement"? I think it was Floyd, who also said, "While perched on the highest barber chair in the world, never forget that you are still sitting primarily on your own behind."

In my opinion, man from time to time should settle back on his own behind and enjoy a thick onion sandwich, perhaps garnished with whiskered white radishes. A sandwich like that tends to clear your head, and I am sure that it also reduces your risk of heart attack and apoplexy, too, whatever apoplexy is.

One of God's unintended consequences of sending us a goodly supply of Wessington Hills onions was that the marble-eyed cattle munching on the buffalo grass that grew on those ancient hills would occasionally wade into a patch of wild onions, and they didn't know the difference.

I am pretty sure that creameries then didn't do to milk what they do to milk these days. And we'd pour that unprocessed milk over our cold oatmeal in the mornings during the spring of the year when the onion crop was just emerging from the ground. I do enjoy a good onion, as I've mentioned, but onion-flavored milk on oatmeal is another thing altogether.

Kids attending rural schools in the days when kids actually walked to school would always find a few wild onions poking up in the ditches on their way to the little white one-roomers that dotted the rural landscape back then.

The early-spring onions would be incorporated into our noon lunches. They seemed to put a little more zip in the lard sandwiches in the lunch bucket. But as the school room warmed up in the afternoon, the smell of chalk and sweating children, most wearing yesterday's underwear, would often be mixed in with the aroma of vaporized onions.

But putting up with onion-flavored milk and school onion breath was a small price to pay for card-carrying onion lovers like myself.

Clifford:

Saw lots of old friends today in Elkton at the big hoedown, but didn't see you. Are you sick? Will you be in town next Saturday. I have a present for you. I must be getting old. Saw some classmates and couldn't remember names. Didn't forget your name, did I?

Matilda Jensen

POST CARD

Clifford Torgusen
RR 4 Ward SD

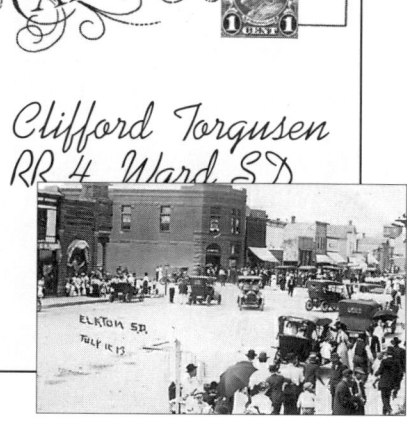

Chapter 4

Names in the Lot

Dyslexia is never having to say you're yrros.

But that really isn't my excuse for having created, from mysterious, invisible strands of ethereal filaments, the name of a fictitious Brookings mayor.

Writing about the whereabouts of the WW II honor roll board of servicemen and women, I flat-out invented and then injected a Mayor Homer Givens into the mix. There was a Homer Givens in town. But he was never our mayor.

I intended to quote Mayor Homer Dwiggins. My apologies to the memories of both of these very good men. How do errors such as this happen? Well, I'll tell you, since I make name mistakes frequently. I'm an expert at it, and I'm often called to lecture on the subject, although I always forget the name of the school where I'm scheduled to appear.

In average people, there's this small area in the brain that's most likely made up of tendrils, gray matter, mycorrhizaea, and microscopic electrical outlets. I also think there is a good chance you'll find a dash of cumin in there, and maybe a pinch of parsley flakes, too.

These ingredients are all massed on the left side of the brain. It's where humans store the names of everyone they meet on their journey through life.

Think of that portion of the brain as a parking lot. Filling it up with names starts with "Mama" quickly followed by "Papa." From there, the parking lot fills quickly and grows to about the size of a barn door before you depart gently into that good night.

Forty-year-olds won't understand this, but anyone over fifty will.

As I envision the brain's parking lot, there are tiny micro-stalls, probably outlined with glow-in-the-dark paint. You meet someone new, you steer the name into the lot, spot an empty micro-stall, and you park it there for future reference. In a lifetime, that means you'll be filling thousands and thousands of stalls with new names.

If you are a Type A person, well organized and keeping up with your surroundings, you put the names in sections in your parking lot. Ron Smith, for example, would go over there in the "RS" section of the lot. Waldemore Weaverstad (an old newspaper editor I once knew) ends up way down at the end in the "WW" section.

Burdened with these thousands of names, you are ready to attend your high school class reunion, go to church, run for office, or meet a familiar face on the street. The way it is supposed to work is that in nanoseconds your brain hits an ignition switch, the name is driven out on squealing tires, and you are able to blurt out, "Teddy Toothache, is that you?"

Politicians are good at organizing their brains' name parking lots. Gov. Ralph Herseth, whom I will talk about in another chapter of this little book, was an expert at remembering names. He not only had a huge parking lot where he placed the names, but was able to park them so expertly that there was also room left between the glowing tape on the pavement for other details, such as what their children's names were.

Type D people like me aren't able to establish good parking lots or to maintain them after we get something similar to a lot established in our otherwise nimble brains. The glow-in-the-dark paint has faded, many of the lot's security lights are missing their bulbs, and some interlopers have managed to sneak in the back way and park illegally without my knowledge. I have no idea who they are or where they came from.

My name lot is, frankly, as messy as a hog house. The names are jammed into little spaces helter-skelter, like carnival bumper cars after a power outage.

Some names collide and a letter or two flies out, sticking in a name parked in another space. Mike Smith might become Mike Allen and Bob Allen becomes Mike Smith.

There are other names in the lot that I've carelessly double-parked and some that I've unwisely put up on blocks. A couple are being cannibalized for parts.

With that in mind, I hope you can now understand how the late Homer Givens of Brookings, who was once Executive Director of the South Dakota Newspaper Association, was mistakenly assigned the job Homer Dwiggins once had. Twice.

And to set this mayor business straight once and for all, I need to notify City Hall. I'll just give the mayor a call. Let's see now, I think his name is Virgil Homer, or is it Givens Dwiggins? Or Waldemore Weaverstad?

 February Postcards

Feb. 3, 1927: W. C. Nelson won first place in a coffee drinking contest at the Centerville American Legion post today, drinking fifty-six cups of java.

Feb. 3, 1891: Edgar McFadden, who would gain fame with his development of the first rust-resistant wheat strain, was born today in Day County. His new strain would appropriately be called Hope Wheat.

Feb. 4, 1887: After a blizzard delayed shipment of newsprint to Mound City in Campbell County, the local *Journal* printed this week's issue on brown wrapping paper borrowed from a local store.

Feb. 4, 1933: A dairy farmer was killed while trying to run a roadblock during the Farmers Holiday strike near Jefferson today.

Feb. 6, 1928: A missing alligator was captured today in the Fall River at Hot Springs by a passing mail carrier. The gator had escaped from a tank at the South Dakota Soldiers Home in June of 1927. It had been sent as a gift to Jack Richards, a resident in the home, by a man in Florida. Before escaping captivity, the gator measured twenty-one inches long. It fared well in the wild and managed to not only survive, but to grow by ten inches in the naturally warm Fall River water.

Feb. 6, 1933: Movie star Mamie VanDoren was born Jean Olander today in Rowena.

Feb. 6, 1940: National television anchorman Tom Brokaw was born today in Webster.

Feb. 8, 1881: The fourteenth session of the Dakota Territorial Legislature approved a bill establishing the penitentiary at Sioux Falls today. Cost was not to exceed $50,000.

Feb. 8, 1888: In the town of Carbonate near Lead, miner John Tripp stepped into an Iron Hill mine shaft at the two hundred-foot level of the mine and fell to his death to a depth of four hundred feet.

Feb. 10, 1892: A. H. Montgomery of the Interstate Artificial Rain Company met with farmers from Davison, Aurora, Jerauld, Brule, Douglas, and Charles Mix Counties and offered to make it rain for a fee of $500, which was raised. It didn't rain.

Feb. 11, 1925: The National Ski Association of America opened its twenty-second annual ski tournament today in Canton, where a wooden ski jump ramp had been constructed.

Feb. 11, 1957: Laura Ingalls Wilder, author of *The Little House on the Prairie* and other popular books, died today near Mansfield, MO.

Feb. 11, 1858: Rose Otto Sayer, who was known in northeastern South Dakota as Rose of the Prairie, was born today. She became a successful farmer in Day County and so loved her buggy horse Kit that she had the horse buried at her eventual gravesite so they could be together in death.

Feb. 11, 1926: The Board of Directors of Drammer Hall in Elkton today barred some of the new dances and posted notice that the Flee Hop, Charleston, cheek-to-cheek, and other improper dancing "is hereby barred."

Feb. 12, 1945: A balloon bomb launched in Japan weeks earlier as a terror weapon during WW II exploded near Norlin, SD.

Feb. 13, 1943: The state legislature approved a bill making the pheasant, first introduced in the state in 1912, the official state bird.

Feb. 13, 1901: Annie D. Tallent, first white woman in the Black Hills, arriving there in 1874, died today in Sturgis.

Feb. 15, 1899: A cottage at the Yankton State Hospital burned today, killing seventeen patients.

Feb. 16, 1869: The Senate ratified the 1868 treaty with the Sioux Indians, giving them the Black Hills, among other territories. Pres. Jackson would sign the bill on Feb. 24, 1869.

Feb. 16, 1910: Some Spearfish business people are investigating Devil's Tower to determine the commercial value of its granite, believed to be worth millions of dollars. The tower is of basalt.

Feb. 17, 1881: William Donaldson, representing Deuel County at the fourteenth Dakota Territorial Legislature meeting in Yankton, announced from the floor the birth of a daughter named Minerva. The delegates immediately voted to purchase a gift for the new arrival, and a gold-lined sterling cup appropriately engraved was purchased. Minerva later gave the cup to the State Museum in Pierre.

Feb. 17, 1925: Mrs. Alice Hewitt of Wakonda received a patent today for a moth-proof clothes cabinet with special joints in the top and bottom of the doors.

Feb. 17, 1936: The coldest temperature in the state to this date, fifty-eight below zero, sent shivers through residents of McIntosh.

Feb. 17, 1853: Alice Ivers Tubbs, better known as Poker Alice, was born today in Sudbury, Devonshire, England.

Feb. 18, 1944: Future South Dakota governor George S. Mickelson made his first appearance before the South Dakota House of Representatives at age four today. When he was born in 1941, a Legislative Resolution gave him the middle name of "Speaker" in honor of his father.

When George S. Mickelson was born in 1941, a legislative resolution gave him his middle name, Speaker, in honor of his father, who was at that time Speaker of the House and who later became Governor. In this photograph, George Speaker, in the center, standing at the podium in the South Dakota House of Representatives, O. H. Hove, Speaker of the House, and at right, Mrs. Madge Mickleson. *Mickelson Family Photo*

Feb. 18, 1924: The second set of triplets born in South Dakota to date arrived at the Ole and Anna Buvick farm in White Township, Marshall County. The girls were named Margaret, Mary, and Margie.

Feb. 19, 1892: John Lehman finally became the first man legally hanged in South Dakota for the 1884 murder of Constable John Barnes near Fairburn. Governors had stayed the execution twice, but public outcry prevailed, and Lehman was finally hanged in Custer.

Feb. 21, 1943: John Perrett, aka Potato Creek Johnny, who came to the Black Hills from Wales when he was 17, died today in Deadwood.

Feb. 22, 1934: Major League Baseball manager Sparky Anderson was born today in Bridgewater. He would become the only manager to take teams from both the American and National Leagues to World Series titles.

Feb. 22, 1889: The Enabling Act was passed today providing for the admission of South Dakota, North Dakota, Montana, and Washington to the Union.

Feb. 23, 1931: In one of the earliest springs on record, pasque flowers bloomed today in the Wessington Hills near Wessington Springs, but the following summer would burn hot and dry as the Dust Bowl continued.

Feb. 24, 1896: Fifty leading citizens of Mitchell, including four of the town founders, sacked and burned the newspaper office of the

Mitchell Mail today for what they perceived to be attacks upon them, their friends, and the town of Mitchell by the *Mail*. Controversial editor-publisher Robert MacBride saw the crowd coming and hid in the Warne Drug Store.

Feb. 26, 1920: O. R. VanEtten of Hyde County, a member of the last Territorial Legislature and the man who introduced House Bill 55, which struck the word "male" from South Dakota election laws, died today at 84.

Feb. 26, 1939: Famous Hollywood actor Robert Gleckler, a native of Pierre, died today in California. He had just been cast to play the part of the overseer in the film epic, *Gone With The Wind*.

Feb. 27, 1909: A Vermillion seed house shipped a consignment of twenty bushels of white seed corn to Russia today.

Feb. 27, 1889: The Milwaukee Railroad sold tickets in Armour, SD, today for round trip, first class trips to the Inauguration of William Henry Harrison in Washington, D. C. Cost was $35.25.

Feb. 29, 1956: A meteorite fell through the roof of a machine shed on the Malcolm McMurchie ranch near Centerville today, said to be the first time that something from outer space struck a man-made object in South Dakota.

TUCK'S POST CARD
CARTE POSTALE.

POSTKARTE.

By Appointment.

Raphael Tuck & Sons' *"Yuletide"* SERIES OF POST CARDS, Nº 104.

Printed in England.

ART PUBLISHERS TO THEIR MAJESTIES THE KING AND QUEEN.

(FOR ADDRESS ONLY.)

Hi grandma and grandpa:
We had our school picnic this
week and I won the marble
game. School is out in two
days. I am happy.
Your grandson
Emil

(Mother—Emil ask me to
write this note to you. Sally.
That's his school on back of
card)

Mr. and Mrs. Clyde Calvin
RR 3, Box 54

Chapter 5

Marbles

Sad as it may seem, youngsters today have pretty much lost their marbles.

Or they probably never had any to begin with.

But here on the flatlands during the bare dirt days from the 1920s through the '40s, the little boy game of marbles was the cat's meow and a sunny afternoon's entertainment all rolled into one.

Boys spoke of dibs, immies, and mibs, and hoarded their marble collections in draw-string bags their mothers made. They hauled more of them to school and around the neighborhood in bulging pockets. Marbles of various genealogies and vast numbers were neighborhood symbols of social status and athletic prowess. The thumb and knuckle kids anxiously waited all winter long for the ground to dry in the spring.

The object with marbles was to humble one's opponents, to be sure. But the real attraction was to keep what one had and capture even more puries, steelies, cat's eyes, and those ubiquitous, dime-a-dozen glassies. It was a game where arguments were few. There was an enviable code of honor among marble players. You either hit or you missed a marble. Close didn't count except at the lag line.

Most men with gray hair and Social Security numbers beginning with zero remember the meandering, after school walks home playing "chase." At about the last step below the school door, the first player would toss his marble in the general direction of home. The other players in turn flipped their best marbles in that direction, too. After each had tossed his shooter, the procedure was repeated again and again all the way home, although the lagging distances would often vary depending on target range. If a shooter hit another shooter's marble, he won a marble from that opponent.

The game of "chase" eventually got you home. But the real heavy hitting, gutsy, gambling game of marbles was played out on plots of dirt hastily cleared of rocks and other encumbrances. Before lawns and big parking lots, finding a battlefield was easy. On somewhat level ground, a circle three or four feet in diameter was scratched out. Then the boys of spring got down and dirty on one knee or two, depending upon individual style, for the mother of all marble games.

Preliminary negotiations included a lag line to determine order of play and what the original ante of marbles into the circle would be. Glassies were the usual trading stock herded into the circle. They were as common as runny noses and were also called dibs, hoodles, kimmies, immies, or just plain mibs. Perhaps to put some spice in the game, each player would be required to add a really nice marble, such as an aggie, made of agate, or a steelie, a steel ball bearing that was a bear to knock from the circle. Steelies were the heavy tanks of our marble wars.

Shooting in lag line order, players knuckled down just outside the circle and fired at the herd of marbles clustered sheepishly in the center. Marbles knocked from the circle were the shooters' to keep. A lucky hit could mean several marbles.

Marbles, although solidly struck, sometimes didn't roll out of the circle. They remained perhaps inches from the circle's border, easy pickings for the next shooter.

Another game where a kid could lose it all in minutes was called "pot." One or more small holes the size and depth of a drinking glass were scooped into the dirt. An agreed-upon number of each player's marbles were placed inside each hole.

Toeing a lag line perhaps ten feet away, players tossed or rolled marbles at the pots. If the shooter's marble fell into the pot, he became a marble millionaire.

Firing off a marble required practice and a talented thumb. Beginners held the orb limply in the bend of the index finger. The thumb flipped it out feebly and inaccurately.

Neighborhood pros balanced the marble in the crook of the index finger with the marble up against the thumbnail. With the index knuckle on the ground for traction, they squeezed off their missiles with unbelievable speed and accuracy. The cracking sound of marble on marble was like a pistol shot. A good power shooter could break another's precious marble.

It is believed that marbles have been around for centuries. There is evidence that Greeks and Romans played games with marbles two thousand years ago.

After WW II and the coming of television, marbles began to lose favor. The big U.S. marble companies lost interest and income as Japanese marble makers entered the fray. They introduced the popular "cat's eye" marble, a clear sphere with what appeared to be a cat's eye of many colors at the center.

Today, it is unlikely that many youngsters wear out the knees of their britches, scuff the toes of their shoes, have permanently dirt-stained knuckles, or sport pockets bulging with marbles locked and loaded for instant combat.

In a manner of speaking, society has indeed lost its marbles.

POST CARD

Place the Stamp here
ONE CENT

Hello from Chicago. Big place, big buildings, big wheels, send money. Will catch train tonight for Aunt Myrna's, then head for home. Do you miss me?

Gerald

Mr. and Mrs. Leo Harms
Elkton PO #34

Michigan Boulevard, Chicago.

Chapter 6

K-Mart Salaries

If we'd called for a vote on it down at Cook's Cafe at 6 a.m. some morning, the guys woulda voted it down.

We're talking about the unbelievable salaries some chief executives are being paid these days.

In particular, we'd like to have the folks who managed the national KMart chain join us sometime for a lesson or two on good judgment and on just exactly what a hard-earned dollar really is.

I don't know about you, but reading about the firm's decision to close hundreds of its stores in South Dakota and other states as it tailspins into bankruptcy gave me a bad case of apoplexy. The salaries they were paying their top guys were, to put it mildly, obscene.

Where do boards of directors find these ya-hoos who oversee their businesses anyway? Is there a "blue-light special" management school somewhere that trains people on how to not live in the real world?

The chief guy at KMart, who should be required to pay it all back, was making about $1.2 million a month. A month? Hello? And to rub salt in the wound, all he managed to do was help the company lose its KMart keester.

His assistant, who was another financial wizard, made $14 million from KMart's non-existent profits in less than two years.

I don't know about you, but I have yet to meet a manager or chief executive or an assistant anywhere who is worth $1 million a month. In fact, I have yet to meet anyone who is worth even a $1 million salary a year.

Perhaps since the South Dakota Legislature is debating a proposed law to control gas prices, they should amend it to set a limit on what chief executive officers can make, too.

Here in my hometown of Brookings, down around the table at Cooks, we figure that these KMart guys (and the rest that are paid those out-of-the-universe salaries we read so much about) soon reach a point where they have no concept of what a hard-earned dollar actually is. How could they when they make $1.2 million a month?

If KMart would give us at the round table just six months as advisors, I will guarantee the owners and the board of directors that the firm will not lose money. And we won't charge them millions for our management expertise, either.

For starters, we'd take the money paid to top management and raise the pay of the folks out in the trenches, in the storerooms and narrow aisles and at the cash registers. They make or break a business. This is not rocket science. Everyone should know that.

We at the breakfast round table come from the old school. We know what a hard-earned dollar really is.

A story about my family's old goat might help explain good management and hard-earned dollars.

I asked my dad before he died about that old goat we once had when I was growing up in Wessington Springs. I remember it whiling away the hours of late summer at the far end of a frayed rope, lollygagging around a stubby, thirsty elm tree that was not long for the world.

The Depression was still stirring up dust devils and difficulties out here on the flatlands. Times were as tough as shoe leather.

He bought the goat, my dad said, because he was going north for a few weeks with a combine crew to earn a few extra hard-earned dollars.

The goat would provide us kids with a daily dose of milk harvested by my mother. My dad made $4 a week working at the elevator, and he spent half a week's pay on that stubborn old goat.

My dad had a good, real-world head on his broad shoulders. But Kmart never invited him to serve on their board.

Before Dad left for North Dakota, he gave us kids and my mother detailed lessons on the care and feeding of that mangey old bleater. He showed my mother how to milk it from the back while on her knees. He showed us kids how to hold the goat's front end.

Later, we moved up in the world. We got a cow.

But during all of their lives, my parents raised four kids and earned just a few hard-earned dollars. I doubt if it came anywhere close to $1 million despite both parents working at menial jobs for long hours. When my mother died at 94, her estate was only $8,600, all of it comprised of very hard-earned dollars.

Never in their wildest dreams, nor in your parents' wildest dreams either, would anyone then have thought that at the beginning of this new century, some over-blown, tassel-shoed fancy-dans at KMart or other similar stores would make thousands of dollars an hour. And not only that, but earn it while running a business into bankruptcy.

So will someone please tell me where I can reach the KMart Board of Directors?

I'll invite them to Brookings for breakfast at Cooks where the guys and gals at every table and booth, all making hard-earned dollars, will be more than happy to advise the board about what went wrong at KMart and how to fix it.

It's not that difficult. You only spend the hard-earned dollars that you have, and you never pay managers millions a year.

I think every big business needs to have an old goat on a frayed rope. One of the duties of every chief executive would be to kneel down behind it once a day and milk that goat until it was bone dry.

That experience and that view would bring them back to the real world and to hard-earned dollars in a big hurry.

March Postcards

March 1, 1877: Jack McCall, who shot Wild Bill Hickok in the back while he was playing poker in Deadwood's Saloon Number 10, was hanged today in Yankton.

March 1, 1954: Catherine Bach, star of television's Dukes of Hazard, was born today in Ohio but grew up in Faith.

March 3, 1931: "The Star Spangled Banner" was designated the National Anthem. In 1893 at Ft. Meade near Sturgis, the post commander's wife suggested that the song be played each evening at post retreat and at the close of parades and concerts. So well accepted was the tradition that in 1914 the Army ordered every post to play the song at retreat. This led to its being selected as the national anthem.

March 4, 1916: Three died when a southbound Dakota Central morning train to Sioux Falls crashed through a fire-weakened bridge north of Thomas in Hamlin County.

March 4, 1890: Seth Bullock and other Deadwood cowboys visiting in Washington, D. C., had lunch with Pres. Teddy Roosevelt today.

March 5, 1903: The pasque flower, usually the first flower to bloom each South Dakota spring, was designated the official state flower.

Famous rodeo cowboy Casey Tibbs at Crystal Springs Rodeo, Clear Lake. *Chuck Cecil Photo*

March 5, 1929: Casey Tibbs, who became a world champion rodeo cowboy, winning the national champion bronc title six times and twice named the nation's all-around cowboy, was born today on his parents'

Cheyenne River homestead near Pierre. During his career, Tibbs suffered the following broken bones: jaw, ribs, arm, vertebra, hip, leg, foot, ankle, hand, and shoulder.

March 6, 1883: A Christmas package mailed for the 1882 Christmas at the McPherson County homestead of James Hart arrived by mail today.

March 6, 1941: Gutzon Borglum, the sculptor who created Mt. Rushmore, suffered a fatal heart attack today in Chicago. He was 74.

Sculptor Gutzon Borglum inspecting Mt. Rushmore. *Bell Photo*

March 7, 1878: A memorable storm hit the Black Hills today with snow drifting to second story windows in Deadwood. An empty hay wagon onto which snow had drifted was later weighed and was found to be carrying 3,165 pounds of snow.

March 7, 1884: Harvey Dunn, famous prairie artist, was born on his parents' homestead near Manchester today.

March 9, 1971: Frank S. Johnson, Pierpont blacksmith and proud owner of the first ever acetylene torch in Day County, died today.

March 10, 1947: The Black Hills Spruce was named the state's official tree.

March 10, 1889: The first church service by a minister was held today in Harding County. Officiating was Rev. Sempler of the Rapid City Presbyterian Church.

March 11, 1950: Charles A. Windolph, who received the Medal of Honor for bravery under fire as a member of the 7th Cavalry's "H" troop at Little Big Horn, died today in Lead. His horse played out as Custer led his men into battle and Windolph joined other soldiers on Reno Hill. He braved enemy fire several times, rushing to the nearby Little Big Horn river to fetch water for the dug-in troops on the hill.

March 12, 1901: L. G. Saunders, who would become a pilot and an Air Force general, was born today near Stratford. He was placed in charge of the top secret war effort to organize and train the first pilots of a B-29 bombing group that would later drop the atomic bomb on Japan.

March 14, 1903: Pres. Theodore Roosevelt's train passed through Tripp today, and during a two-minute stop, Teddy addressed a crowd at the station.

March 15, 1928: A whistle officially announced the end of the town of Cambria in the Black Hills today. The high-grade coal that had been mined there ran out, and the company announced that unless new coal was discovered by this date, a whistle would announce the end of Cambria, population 1,400.

March 15, 1943: Abram West, of Savo Township near Fredrick, died today. As a young man in 1875, he worked in the Rainbow Gold Mine in Placer, CA, and became famous for panning a gold nugget worth $11,200.

March 15, 1954: Pres. Dwight D. Eisenhower flipped the switch today sending power through lines stretching out from the Missouri River's Ft. Randall Dam on the Missouri River.

March 19, 1884: Famous author Hamlin Garland was in line today waiting to receive a receipt for the $200 he paid for his homestead claim near Leola.

March 20,1988: Amanda (Mandy) Clement, professional baseball's first female umpire, was born today in Hudson. She would later be elected to the Baseball Hall of Fame in Cooperstown, NY.

March 20 1903: Almond Pederson of Toronto was chosen as the first Rural Free Delivery (RFD) mailman out of that Deuel County community. His route would be thirty miles long and he would receive $500 a year.

March 21, 1849: John Spaulding, aka Buckskin Johnny, was born today in Wisconsin. He would become a popular guide for wagon trains headed for the Black Hills, and he later built one of the first homes in Butte County.

March 22, 1883: Deuel County inventor Sheldon Washburn was born today near Goodwin. In 1946 he received a patent on a beamless plow. He was the first South Dakotan to build a snowmobile and one of the first to install a cab on his farm tractor.

March 22, 1920: When a blizzard struck at his ranch south of Red Elm, John Leber personally carried, one by one, 450 head of sheep across a thawed out creek to a shelter on the opposite side of the creek. So much snow later drifted into the three-sided shelter that when he later checked on the flock, they had packed down snow until their backs touched the top of the shelter.

March 23, 1910: An Arizona man claimed today that Wild Bill Hickok was not buried in Deadwood. The former pony express rider claimed he was with Wild Bill when he was shot. He said Wild Bill was originally buried in Deadwood, but a flood a year later uncovered the grave and the body was then taken to Washington for reburial. Deadwood old timers denied the story, claiming it was a hoax. Wild Bill's body was exhumed in 1878 for viewing by a female carnival owner who claimed that she was his wife, they said. The body was also viewed by several others and then placed back in the grave at Deadwood.

March 24, 1897: A hog that sought shelter between two haystacks near Tripp during a blizzard emerged today after over seventy days beneath the snow bank. It was described by the farmer-owner this way: "All before the ears is nose and all behind the ears is tail."

March 24, 1921: About two hundred farmers, all deputized and armed with shotguns and rifles, today stood guard over 330 cows donated for German children by Russian-German farmers in Hutchinson County. Anti-German ruffians who were against using the cows for this purpose came to the pasture about 10:30 a.m., but being badly outnumbered, left.

March 25, 1926: Hyde County Sheriff Lee McNamara was shot and killed today by George Meservey, who ranched in northwest Hyde County. Meservey was being evicted from his home through foreclosure when he fired the fatal shot. He was sentenced to life in prison.

March 26, 1881: The ice break-up on the upper Missouri River floated downstream and destroyed the city of Vermillion, then located along its banks.

March 26, 1886: Archille LaGuardia, conductor of the Army band at Ft. Sully, south of what is now Pierre, presented the last concert for the fall and winter season at the fort today, with a piece by Verdi. The director's son Fiorella was at the fort at that time. He later became mayor of New York, serving from 1933 to 1945.

March 27, 1899: Near Manila, The Philippines, South Dakota's 1st Regiment, Volunteer Infantry, charged the enemy, and nine troopers were killed.

March 27, 1908: Well drillers sank their first oil well today near South Shore in Codington County. Five months later, work was abandoned, but the search for oil in that area continued on and off through 1957.

March 28, 1906: The Couch Line Railroad, said to be the world's crookedest rail line, was completed today from Rapid City to Mystic. The line clung to high cliffs, and, in the valleys, crossed creeks 105 times in its twenty-six-mile length.

March 29, 1918: Sam White Bear became the first Native American from the Pine Ridge Reservation to die in WW I service at Camp Cody, NM, during training.

March 30, 1743: A message on what became known as the Verendryes Plate was carved on a piece of lead eight and one-half by six and one-half inches by four French explorers and left on a hill near Ft. Pierre.

March 31, 1904: Citizens in the town of Miller in Hand County welcomed electric lights into their homes today.

SOUTH DAKOTA STATE
CAPITOL, PIERRE.

Miller Studio Pic.

Ralph Herseth
Governor.

Chapter 7

Campaiging 1950s Style

The old motel is still there, at the back of a big gravel lot. It's just west of the Lake Preston High School which you pass by as you throttle down to abide by the city's twenty-five mile per hour speed limit on Highway 14 through town.

For fifty years, each time I've driven by that flat-roofed, 1950s motel, memories of my introduction to South Dakota politics and political campaigning in 1958 come flooding back. Ralph Herseth, the Democratic candidate for governor that year, hired me out of the college classroom to assist in his campaign. I was a neophyte at campaiging and, for that matter, at politics, having had no interest whatsoever in that subject when Ralph and I sat down in an empty journalism building classroom for our brief interview one spring day.

He hired me despite my lack of political moxy, and we became joined at the hip out on the long campaign trail, traveling over 25,000 miles together in a boxy station wagon loaded down with campaign lit-

This was the official campaign photograph used in Ralph Herseth's campaign. It appeared on most of his literature, including large window posters.
Herseth Family Photo

erature. No other candidate in that 1958 campaign would log more South Dakota miles on highways or in the air. We would campaign a total of sixty-four days, often six days a week. Ralph had a policy of always being home at his ranch with his family every Sunday, although on a few occasions, campaign events dictated otherwise.

We visited nearly every South Dakota community and dozens of city and state parks. We stopped in far-off Harding County twelve miles from the North Dakota border and at a little wide spot in eastern South Dakota called, appropriately, Ralph, where Ralph told me he had made his first speech as a gubernatorial candidate. After that initial speech, Ralph spoke to crowds as small as seven who gathered at a country store in a town whose name now escapes me. His largest and most enthusiastic audience was his speech at the Democratic Convention in the old Lincoln Hotel in Watertown on July 21. That old hotel, now razed, had been virtually closed that summer, but the management opened up all five floors for the convention. Every room was filled. It was the old five-story hotel's swan song, and it closed soon after the convention ended.

The campaign trail

We traveled smooth, broad highways and rough washboard roads, meeting potential voters in venues ranging from muddy feedlots to auction barns to fancy hotel banquet rooms and church basements through the summer and fall of 1958. Ralph rode in dozens of town parades observing the Fourth of July or a high school homecoming. I followed his parade route on the sidewalk, handing out literature and trying to keep up, dodging the crowds along the way. Once, we arrived late at the State Corn Picking Contest in Moody County near Flandreau. We didn't know the way to the site, but we spotted some campaign signs that read "Herseth Leads The Way." We followed them and, sure enough, they led us to the contest.

One night in Winner, we were among the sold-out audience of Democrats waiting for the arrival of Rep. Harold Cooley of North Carolina, who was the main speaker. Cooley at last notified event planners that he couldn't make the trip. This was just moments before the banquet was to begin. The county chairman announced the bad news to the Democrats who were seated and waiting to be served their ham dinner. They learned that Ralph, who was seated at the head table as a special guest and was not scheduled to speak, would be the substitute keynoter. The audience was told that if they wished they could receive two dollars back from their ticket price, which the audience and Ralph found very amusing. No one asked for a refund, and Ralph did a great job substituting.

Late one night, tired and worn after a day of smiling, shaking hands, and giving speeches, far behind our planned travel schedule and on the road returning to Ralph's home near Aberdeen for a weekend rest, we decided to call it a day. We found that little motel in Lake Preston. It had one small, empty room hardly big enough for the double bed. Ralph was a big man with a generous middle-aged spread. I spent the night clinging to one small sliver along the wall side of that double bed. I was kept awake by the tossing, turning, and snoring of the man who would be governor. It was a long night out on the hustings, and I have always remembered it.

Another night we shared a room in the upstairs bedroom at Brookings County Democratic Chairman Paul Mershon's farm home just west of Greenwood Cemetery in the northwest quadrant of the cemetery road and the first township gravel road west. Paul was remembered as the state deputy sheriff who, during Prohibition days, shot and killed a bootlegger in White, who intended to shoot at him. Paul and Ruby's house is still there, but Paul's huge, picturesque barn was removed long ago. We often stayed at the homes of county chairmen or other loyal Democratic supporters, but usually we were assigned separate rooms. I remember the comfortable apartment barrister Ward Clark had over his law office in downtown Canistota, and the courteous welcome we received in dozens of other homes we stayed in to conserve on our limited campaign budget.

A two-term senator

I can picture Gov. Ralph Herseth in my mind today. He was a handsome man with a full head of white hair and a farmer tan. Ralph was 49 years old at the time and had spent two four-year terms in the South Dakota Senate. He earned his reputation in the Senate as an intelligent, forceful man of integrity, and he often led his fellow Democrats. He was slightly overweight but looked trim as a rodeo bulldogger. He had an enviable talent for remembering people's names. He always looked greeters square in the eye when they stopped him on the street or after an evening meeting to commiserate. He managed a hardware store in

Gov. Ralph Herseth wore many hats. Here, he donned his farmer's hat to oversee construction of a new pole barn on his Houghton ranch.
Herseth Family Photo

Houghton, but his preference was working his Angus ranch. He walked with a slight swaying motion as if one knee wasn't what it should be. He was articulate, personable, very polite and courteous, a down to earth charmer of a guy with a wry smile and twinkle in his eye. He spoke the language of farming and ranching but from his business experience and his Senate years, he also held his own and then some during any discussion of political issues. And he could deliver his message in a booming voice.

As a Democat, his was an uphill struggle in Republican-dominated South Dakota, just as it is today. For years, Democratic legislators in Pierre have joked that they could hold their party caucus in a telephone booth.

But he would overcome the odds and become the first Democrat elected governor since Governor Tom Berry, who served from 1933 to 1937. Herseth was proud of that. He used the decades-long Republican monopoly in the statehouse to his advantage, and his mantra, repeated over and over again during the campaign, was that "it was time for a change." It became what is known today as the thirty-second tag line. His only opposition in the primary election dropped out, which gave him an open road for the candidacy. It was a different time for campaigns. They were quieter and less sophisticated, and there were fewer of the slick television and multi-media promotions. The cadre of high-paid political hacks, speech writers, and hangers on most campaigns now employ hadn't been born. There was much more one-on-one, handshaking contact between candidate and voter. Only once or twice did the state's largest, most influential newspaper, the Sioux Falls *Argus Leader* (which then claimed to serve all of South Dakota), feature candidate stories on their front page. Usually, what candidates said at speeches throughout South Dakota was included in a roundup or amalgamation of all of the campaigns under a two-column headline on an inside page. Even the Democratic state convention in July, where state candidates were officially approved, keynote speeches given, and a platform written, the coverage was relegated to an inside newspaper page of the state's largest newspaper. For a fledgling journalist like me, this was good because although my news stories sent to the *Argus* might have been shortened, the *Argus* printed them basically as I had written them.

Campaigns and the politicians who conducted the campaigns seemed less strident then. The era of the pesky, bothersome telephone campaigns with taped messages automatically operated by computers hadn't been invented. There were no computers for mass mailings of literature. There was far less campaign hype and vitriol, and there were no pointy-headed, alligator-shoed, so-called campaign experts from Washington flying in and out of the state to advise the candidate on what he should say and how he should say it.

Ralph and I were the entire Herseth For Governor campaign staff. Ralph had apparently spoken to someone about his need for an assistant, and it was suggested he speak to Dr. George Phillips, then head of the South Dakota State University Journalism Department. He was looking for someone who could also write a news release, an advertisement, or a brochure. That person would also manage the Aberdeen Herseth for Governor headquarters. Dr. Phillips recommended me for the job. Ralph met me in the Journalism Building on campus and offered me what was an opportunity of a lifetime. I happily accepted his offer. But before it was official, Ralph wanted to run it by the state Democratic Central committee. I'll always remember the interview I had in Watertown with the members of the prestigious state Democratic Central Committee. At the meeting they were all hunkered down for strategic planning in Cobb Chase's plush office on the second floor of the Midland Life Insurance Building just east of the Codington County Courthouse.

Ralph introduced me to the committee, and then Cobb and the others took over. The members sat in chairs that lined the walls of Cobb's office. He was the chief executive of Midland. I didn't know any of the central committee members. I sat uncomfortably in a chair in front of Cobb's battleship-sized walnut desk and tried to relax. I was wearing a cheap suit and tie. I honestly didn't really know if I was a Democrat, a Republican, or if I held any other affiliation. But I wanted the job, and I anointed myself a Democrat in a very big hurry. I would learn later that political affiliation isn't something you just decide to adopt on a moment's notice. It is a deep-seated, philosophical belief that is formed by your life's experiences, I would learn as the years passed by.

I passed the inquisition and prepared to do all that I could to assist Ralph on the arduous mission upon which we were about to depart. I resigned my position as the South Dakota State University *Collegian* editor.

After making final arrangements in Brookings, I packed my belongings, including that new suit and tie, in a small brown and white suitcase made of cardboard that I bought at the Montgomery Ward store in Brookings. Ralph picked me up on one of his campaign swings through Brookings, and I drove the two of us (very carefully, to impress my new boss), back to Aberdeen. We officially opened the campaign office at 20 Third Ave. SE on July 3, 1958. It had previously been the Triangle School Supply store.

I would earn $75 a week plus room and board. The "room" in the campaign headquarters turned out to be a little square cubicle in the cavernous back room. I used my two khaki Navy blankets as walls. They were hung on water pipes arranged "L-shaped" in a back corner of the store. The blankets were held in place with safety pins. An old army bunk was moved in along with a small bedside table and lamp. This would be my home for six months. Our "Herseth For Governor" headquarters was next door to a popular bar in Aberdeen. When I was in town I was often serenaded to sleep by the pounding of the jukebox in the bar's dance floor next door. The good thing about being next to that bar was that every noon, it offered ham slices and beans free to customers. I would buy a 10-cent glass of Coke and eat my lunch for free.

From county fairs to Kiwanis Club meetings

One of our first tasks was to map out a loose daily and weekly plan for Ralph's campaign appearances. We penciled in the obvious appearances, such as the State Fair, the Democratic convention dates at the Lincoln Hotel in Watertown, college and university homecomings, some of the larger county fairs, the Corn Picking contest, and other set events where Ralph could meet protential voters. Our schedule would obviously

PARTNERS FOR PROGRESS

HERSETH FOR GOVERNOR

THE CHOICE

SCHIRMER FOR LT. GOVERNOR

During Ralph Herseth's second run for a two-year term for governor (he was defeated by his good friend Archie Gubbrud), this card was handed out to thousands of protential voters during the campaign. Herseth's running mate was M.E. (Mike) Schirmer of Sioux Falls. Other state and national Democratic candidates on the ticket were listed on the back of the card, including two-term Congressman George McGovern, who was also defeated that year in his bid for the U. S. Senate. He was, however, soon named by Pres. John Kennedy to head up the nation's Food For Peace program. *Herseth Family Photo*

be adjusted as we progressed through the summer and fall. We coordinated our meetings with county chairpersons and planned out our weekly trips so that we could return to Aberdeen and Ralph could keep his promise to be home at his ranch with his family every Sunday.

We also made plans for preparing and printing the fund raising and campaign literature Ralph would need during the campaign. We enlisted local Democratic volunteers to work in the headquarters when we were out of town.

From about mid-June of 1958 through the general election on Nov. 4, I was with Ralph most mornings, noons, and nights. On days when we were on the campaign trail between scheduled meetings, we made side trips to the small towns and byways of South Dakota. We would park the car on the town's main street, and Ralph would work the businesses and the sidewalk crowds, stopping to introduce himself to everyone he met. We often made special trips to spend time with each of his fellow Democratic senators and with Republican senators with whom Ralph had a special friendship.

I helped write speeches, although near the end of the campaign a stock speech with only minor deviations became commonplace. An integral part of our campaign was a small 3x5 file system I kept. It included the names of people he'd met, folks that he should meet, and people to whom he should send thank you notes or some kind of requested information. At meetings, when Ralph stood greeting those who were attending the event, I was always nearby so he could, from time to time, turn and quietly ask me to make a note that Mrs. So-and-So has a daughter living in Rapid City or that John Smith's son just joined the Air Force, or send me on some other errand. On our second trip through a town, as we were driving to the meeting, Ralph would review the notes I'd jotted down on the 3x5-inch cards during the previous visit. If he met Mrs. So-and-So or John Smith again, he could inquire about the daughter in Rapid City or the young man in the Air Force. Often, he'd remember other inconsequential personal asides that hadn't been written down on our card file. I remember once he complimented a lady on chocolate cake that she had made and served on a previous visit. I am very sure that the cake maker cast her vote that fall for Ralph Herseth.

With his advice and help, I wrote his campaign brochures, and one sunny day we spent an afternoon where I also took photographs of him at work on his ranch. I vividly recall one picture of Ralph we used in a brochure of him in work clothes kneeling and holding a bundle of oats.

A popular handout all of the candidates used back then was the business card. It was something to hand to people the candidates met. The cards usually had printed on the back a listing of license plate county prefix numbers. Everyone Ralph met received his business card. We had thousands printed. We also used thousands of heavy cardboard posters with Ralph's photograph on them. These were placed in store front windows and, on slow days out on country roads, Ralph and I would often stop and tack posters on strategically-located telephone poles or fence posts. Some of the posters were stapled to laths with sharpened ends and were among the first yard signs used in South Dakota political campaigns.

A school bus for special events

The Democratic Party owned an old, gaily painted, red, white, and blue school bus. House Candidate George McGovern's name was painted in large letters on each side of the bus, and Ralph received a smaller billing below McGovern's. Often, when county candidates planned a county-wide blitz, we would join the caravan. I was the designated driver on many of these forays to the towns in the county. At each community, candidates would alight and work the main street and the businesses, handing out their ubiquitous business cards. I often drove the bus in the small-town parades, too, and down sleepy main streets during unannounced afternoon visits. The bus was equipped with a loudspeaker, a microphone, and a tape player. After I announced that Democratic candidates were in town I'd play a tape of "Happy Days Are

Here Again," the traditional Democratic theme song from the 1932 campaign of Franklin Roosevelt that was and still is a popular song often played whenever Democrats gather together. We'd remind the people that it was "time for a change" in Pierre after twenty-two years. Even today, I often pass by and recognize the farmstead on Highway 81 between Arlington and Madison which became our emergency port of call one very hot day when the bus developed water pump problems.

Our two-man campaign staff had to be flexible and ready for any contingency. There were always telephone calls to make far into the night as we helped arrange the following day's events. Cell phones had not yet been invented, so the calling had to be from our motel room or during stops throughout the day. What a time saving device cell phones must be for today's political candidates.

Ralph didn't smoke, and to his credit, he courageously put up with my smelly bad habit in the car. Early on we had agreed, or rather Ralph had insisted, that I would hold my smoldering cigarette next to the driver's side wing window as I drove. That way, most of the smoke would theoretically be removed from the car. As a non-smoker now, I am amazed at the ability of cigarette smoke to always find its way to a non-smoker, so I doubt if our wing-window agreement helped much. We seldom had the car radio on as we traveled. Instead, Ralph read, wrote, and reviewed various campaign documents and letters. Often, he used the down time to nap and rest and relax from the rigors of an intense campaign as he watched the world go by our car window.

A stop in Hot Springs

Our campaign stops, usually visiting several communities each day of the week, seem now to all melt together with just a few specific memories of our travels on any particular trip. I do recall a stop we made in the Black Hills near Hot Springs late one afternoon. Ralph had called ahead and made an appointment with Leslie Jensen, the Republican governor from 1937 to 1939. Politics aside, they were very good friends. Gov. Jensen lived along Fall River a few miles from Hot Springs. We spent an hour with Gov. Jensen, lounging in lawn chairs. The conversation was pleasant and interesting. Mrs. Jensen served lemonade as Herseth and Jensen told stories about campaigning and discussed current issues as we sat there in the cool summer shade. I didn't know it at the time, but Gov. Jensen, in his 1936 campaign for office, promised to complete the paving of Highway 14 completely across the state if he was elected. When he was, he made good on the promise. When we left, Gov. Jensen handed Ralph a check, his contribution to Ralph's campaign. Gov. Jensen died about five years later.

On another trip, I recall that Ralph was particularly distressed when he returned to the car after a visit in the homes of Native Americans living in the ramshackle villages of Little Eagle and Bullhead. Leaving those small communities, he commented that few people probably even realized the towns were there, and probably didn't know how desperate the residents were for such basics as food and proper housing. He said they lived in homes no better than the hen house back on the Houghton farm.

It was Ralph's rule that I would never drive faster than fifty-five miles an hour. He felt he would lose votes if we passed other cars, even at the official speed limit. So cars and trucks were constantly passing us as we drove from one appointment to another. There was a positive side to our snail's pace, however. Usually, Ralph received a friendly toot from the passing car's horn, and a wave or thumb's up sign of support. I remember only once when Ralph relented and suggested we speed up a bit. We were running late, on a washboard gravel road north of Wessington Springs. It was plain that at our usual speed, we would be late for an evening banquet in Wessington Springs.

We would soon pay for our speeding indiscretions. As we spewed out a trail of roiling dust in our wake, a chicken sprinted across our path. It didn't quite make it to the other side of the road. We drove on in silence for another mile or so, and then Ralph decided we needed to go back to the farm house so he could apologize to the chicken's owner about the loss.

We turned around, and we were invited into the farm home. Ralph not only apologized for killing the man's chicken, but reached into his back pocket for his billfold and offered to pay damages. The farmer would have none of it. He was happy that we stopped and said he was honored to meet Ralph in person. As we drove away toward Wessington Springs, we were certain that Ralph had gained not only the two votes at that farm, but more from the farmer's neighbors who would surely hear about the unexpected visit by the candidate for governor who was concerned about a dead chicken. We were, of course, late for the Wessington Springs meeting. By the time we got there, everyone had eaten. In his speech, Ralph apologized for being late, but to his credit he never mentioned our collision with the chicken to those faithful supporters. Incidentally, after his speech, he was served, of all things, fried chicken.

We had just one close call in our 25,000-mile campaign trip. On Highway 28, heading west and on the big curve at the east end of Lake Poinsett near where an old school house still stands, a driver coming from the lake darted out from the gravel road as we barreled toward him. We managed to slow down, and I doubt if the old man who drove on even realized how close we had all come to disaster. After that incident, Ralph reminded me many times, as we would spot a car approaching the highway on a gravel road, that I should never assume that the driver would stop. He explained that often, after riding a tractor in the field all day at a very slow speed, the high speed of an approaching car on a main highway is underestimated by the tractor driver. He said that the tractor driver might now be the one in the car approaching the main highway we were on. To this day, I always keep a sharp eye when a car approaches a highway crossing.

Often when out on the campaign trail, we would leave the main traveled roads and drive the county or township roads so that Ralph could visit the very small towns. If we passed a farm where someone might be out in the yard working, Ralph would have me stop the car, and he would get out to visit with the surprised farmer. In most small towns we would visit the feed stores and the newspaper shops and the local coffee shops. Ralph would introduce himself to all that he met, and if time permitted, ask the people what they liked or disliked about what state government was doing. I would dutifully follow along with an arm load of brochures and posters and ask store owners if I could place one of our posters in their display windows.

One visit to a newspaper shop in a small, northeast South Dakota town stands out in my mind. We were in tiny Langford and stopped at the office of the *Langford Bugle* newspaper. The owner was alone, working on his press in the dingy, dirty back room. He was slightly intoxi-

Governor Ralph Herseth, second from right, his wife Lorna, second from left, and their daughter, now Mrs. Connie Jacobs of Rapid City, far left, meet the British ambassador and his wife and counsel at the Pierre Airport prior to dinner at the Governor's Mansion in 1960. *Herseth Family Photo*

cated, we quickly discovered. It was a Friday, three days after the normal publication day for the *Langford Bugle*. As we visited with the crusty old printer-editor, an elderly lady peeked in the back room to ask the editor why she hadn't received her *Bugle*. The printer pointed to his broken press and in an unkind, gruff voice told her she'd get her "damned paper" when he got his "damned press fixed." We did not linger long in the shop. Ralph judiciously decided not to introduce himself to the lady as we all left the establishment. We laughed about the incident all the way to Bristol, where Ralph resumed his walking tours up and down Main Street.

When the time came to leave a small town for the next one on our list, it was Ralph's idea to make one final stop at the corner gas station to top off the tank. We usually had gas enough for the trip, but buying gas provided an excuse to meet more potential voters. We did this in nearly every town in which we stopped. At the station, Ralph would visit as the owner pumped the gas, and follow him into the building where there were usually one or two men gathered for gossip and car talk. Ralph would pay his gas bill in cash and introduce himself to everyone in the station. We would leave a poster for the station owner to put in his window, and then head out for the next small town on our circuitous route to that day's Kiwanis club meeting or that evening's dinner meeting in an auditorium or church basement.

The tank was always full

We might stop to fill the tank several times a day, but Ralph felt that it gave him an opportunity to meet a few more potential voters, and it also conveyed the message that he had taken the time to spend some of his money in that small town. We were certain that more than just the station owner and his cronies would soon learn of his stop. The owner would also be more likely to let us place a Herseth for Governor sign in his station's front window. We also tried to time our side trips to small towns so that Ralph could eat breakfasts or lunches or take a coffee break in the small cafés. We had a system that worked very well. I would drop him off at the café we selected, then drive to a nearby pay phone or a telephone at a constituent's home or office. After waiting a few minutes, I'd telephone the café and ask if they could page Ralph Herseth. I could hear the waitress' voice call out above the din of rattling plates, silverware, and the café small talk: "Ralph Herseth, Ralph Herseth, you're wanted on the phone!" Heads would turn when they learned, if they didn't know already, that a celebrity was in their midst, eating the same roast beef noon special that they were. Ralph wasn't entirely comfortable with this campaign device, but I convinced him it was inexpensive advertising for him, and he reluctantly agreed to participate.

Nearly every weeknight and on many Saturday nights, loyal county chairmen or Ralph's friends from his days in the Senate would arrange evening banquets or meetings of some sort. At these events, Ralph spoke for about twenty minutes, using his "time for a change" message that he and I both knew by heart. Ralph always localized his message, too, with a few opening remarks, working in names of some in the audience that we knew well. Before the meeting, while driving to a town, we would discuss events of the day and items that would have local interest or consequences, and he was able to skillfully weave them into his talk as if they were among his main concerns. He discussed, of course, the long tenure the Republicans had in Pierre. He singled out the highway department management (not the employees) and claimed mismanagement. He used dollar figures to point point out how the cost of state government had increased over the past few years, accompanied by an increase in the number of state employees. There were other issues, many of them related to the traditional big government versus the people issues similar to those still argued among Democrats and Republicans today.

He never failed to mention that he was a farmer, if he was speaking east of the river in farm country, or a rancher, if speaking out west. In towns, he was a hardware store owner with main street business experience. He liked to mention the condition of crops and pastures he had observed while we drove to the community meeting. He would tell people that he was so happy to have seen the pastures and the fat cattle grazing on grass that was "belly high," as he put it.

Campaign spelling lesson

While he ate and spoke at small town meetings, I would return to our car parked outside and, using the dome light, write a news story of about three hundred words or so on my rattling old portable typewriter. I took it to the local newspaper and slipped the story under the door. We attempted to localize our stories for the community, county, or area we were visiting. For these late-night news writing sessions I had no one to edit my copy, and it probably showed. I remember once asking Ralph to look over the copy for a brochure I had designed and written. In it I had spelled the word prairie incorrectly. I had it "prarie." Ralph politely and diplomatically suggested that I use the dictionary to insure that I had it spelled right. As he recalled, he told me, a grade school teacher taught him that prairie had "air" in it. Through the years, each time I have written the word "prairie" I think of Ralph's campaign spelling lesson.

Most of the campaigning then was one-on-one or in small groups. There was less reliance on newspaper advertising except in the final days of the campaign. Television advertising was almost non-existent. Television was in its infancy in South Dakota. We saved money for a smattering of television spots, most scheduled for the end of the campaign. Usually, at the evening meetings where Ralph spoke, we felt fortunate if twenty-five or fifty people showed up. With television, we would be reaching unbelievably large audiences. The power and reach of television was just beginning to be realized. But political television commercials then were primitive by today's standards. They were, first of all, grainy black and white, and the sound was not crisp. We were novices at the new medium and not very creative in scripting the spots. We did not use staging or props for Ralph's commercials. He simply sat on a stool or stood looking straight into one camera, reading from a teleprompter.

Our major television push came during the final day of campaigning before election day. After our KELO filming was finished, we chartered an airplane for a flight to Rapid City where another filming to be aired on the only television station west of the river was to be made. When we boarded our two-engine airplane in Sioux Falls, we also loaded up a few cardboard boxes of campaign brochures, including hundreds of those little business cards I mentioned earlier. It all would be obsolete and useless in a few hours. So as we flew across South Dakota, over towns like Miller, Harold, Chamberlain, Wasta, and all of the others in between, we threw out handsful of those brochures and cards, hoping our aim was good and that they fluttered gently down in the towns we passed over. Where they fluttered we had no idea. Today, a candidate doing that would most certainly lose the environmental vote and probably be fined by the Environmental Protection Agency. But protecting the environment then was not much of an issue to voters who had lived through the Dust Bowl and now reaped the benefits of soil and water conservation, which was the hot topic. Spending and using money wisely was our creed, and this was another leftover precept from the 1930s Dust Bowl-Depression era. We considered it to be a very creative way to clear our inventory and to gain votes from people who might pick up the brochure or card falling from the sky.

I'll drink to that

We spent election day at our headquarters in Aberdeen, making telephone calls and preparing for what we hoped would be a victory party that evening in our old paint store headquarters. We felt good about the campaign. The South Dakota poll, sponsored by the *Sioux Falls Argus Leader*, the *Aberdeen American News* and the *Watertown Public Opinion*, had Ralph in the lead, which hadn't always been the case. In early July, the poll had Ralph trailing his opponent, former South Dakota Attorney General Phil Saunders, 48.5 percent to 51.5 percent. But several chocolate cakes and road-killed chickens later, in late October just before the election, Ralph had surged ahead with 51.9 percent of the vote to Saunders' 44.8 percent. The farm vote was particularly strong for Ralph, with 55.8 percent of those polled indicating they favored him, to just 41.3 percent who said they would vote for Saunders. The poll in towns and cities was also close, but in both instances, Saunders held a slim lead of one or two percentage points. We worried, of course, but on election day, we were fairly confident that Ralph was about to make history in his "time for change" quest for control of the statehouse.

After the polls closed on election day, the crowds of Aberdeen supporters and others from throughout the state who wanted to be with Ralph began to arrive at headquarters. The place soon became packed with supporters and other hangers on. It was an enjoyable evening for all, especially as the returns declared Ralph the winner.

Old friends and politicians stopped by throughout the evening to congratulate Ralph as the results came in. As victory became more certain, I noticed that often on this important night, Ralph and some of his cronies from the area and from his Legislative days would disappear into the back room into my little plumber-piped, blanket-walled bedroom for a few minutes. I assumed that they were seeking privacy to discuss aspects of governing the state, talk about possible political appointees and political plums, and plan for the upcoming legislative session. This was no doubt the case, but I would learn there was another reason for those backroom visits when I turned in after everyone had left the headquarters that evening. The vote count had Ralph garnering 108,042 votes to Phil Saunders' 99,825. After twenty-two years, a Democrat had finally made it out of the telephone booth and into the governor's office.

After everyone had left, I locked the front door and climbed into my bed, looking forward to a good night's sleep after a long, grueling campaign. The pressure was off, and we had been rewarded for our hard work. I felt something under my pillow. It was a nearly empty pint bottle of good whiskey. Ralph neither smoked nor drank; at least I had never seen him with anything other than coffee or a soft drink in his hand. But during that happy night, one of his old legislative or campaign cronies must have brought the bottle to the party. And during those numerous trips back to my little blanket-clad adobe, Ralph and his friends must have celebrated with a toast or two. But it was only a pint bottle, and it wasn't empty, so the imbibing must have been slight.

After that very successful election resulting in what was an unexpected upset of the party that had been entrenched in power for so long,

Governor Ralph Herseth in late 1950 with capitol dome in the background. *Herseth Family Photo*

as we packed away the campaign paraphernalia, Ralph and I talked about the part I might have in his administration. Being young and confident, and knowing Ralph as I did, I assumed that I would be the logical choice to serve as his administrative assistant. I mentioned that I would welcome the opportunity to serve in that capacity. He said he would think about it, and I headed back to college to sit out the remainder of the quarter awaiting the start of another term after the Christmas holiday. Aside from taking part in his Inaugural in January of 1959, I didn't see or talk to Ralph for several weeks. But one day he called, and we met in a booth at the Pheasant Café in Brookings.

Good gubernatorial advice

There, over a hamburger, he said that he would very much like to hire me as his assistant, but that in thinking it over, he felt it was better that I continue my college studies and graduate. He promised that after I graduated he would have a place for me somewhere in his administration. I was disappointed, of course, but in hindsight, it was very good advice. He hired radio man Max Witcher, a man I didn't know and a name that hadn't come up during the campaign, as his chief aide.

A few weeks before I graduated from SDSU in 1959 with a degree in journalism, I called Ralph and reminded him that I would soon be ready to go to work for him. He called me back a few hours later and told me he was appointing me as the Assistant Director of Highway Publicity, which is now the state Travel and Tourism Department. I would be working under former Springfield (SD) newspaper publisher John Whalen. Coincidentally, long after I had graduated, later in my career which included the position of University Editor at South Dakota State University, I would hire and work with his son, John, Jr., who still lives in Brookings.

My wife Mary and I were married in July 1959. We moved to Pierre shortly thereafter with our few belongings stuffed in the back seat of the car. The new job of promoting South Dakota travel was interesting and exciting. Then, the publicity office was in the Highway Department Building. Despite the joy of working with the national press and others in promoting travel to South Dakota, I missed the newspaper business, having been introduced to it while working part time for the *Brookings Register* as a student. I heard that a job was open at the *Watertown Public Opinion* and, on a whim, I applied.

I drove to Watertown for an interview with the paper's venerable editor, Percy Albrook, a lanky, Ichabod Crane type whom I came to respect as a newspaperman. After our interview, Percy offered me the job as Farm Editor at $90 a week. I told him that if I accepted I would be taking a "large cut in salary." I was currently making $100 a week in Pierre working for the state, you see. Percy decided that he might be able to get $93 a week for me, but that would be pushing the envelope. He left the office to discuss the additional $3 a week offer he'd made with the publisher, Kenny Way, a wonderful man whose family owned the newspaper and considerable property in Watertown's downtown district, plus other property around nearby Lake Kampeska. After a time, Percy returned to the office, sat down, and to my relief said that he "guessed he could pay me $93." But he was quick to remind me that my salary would be more than the *Public Opinion* had ever paid a starting reporter. Mary and I moved from Pierre to Watertown in about two weeks. Since Ralph was busy being governor and had more important gubernatorial duties to perform than to be bothered with my career change and my hurried departure from the Highway Department, I decided not to inform him of my resignation. When he learned of it a few days later, I received a phone call from him. He was not happy that I had left without informing him. I apologized, and that was the last time the two of us ever spoke.

In the next election, Ralph campaigned against a fellow farmer, Republican Archie Gubbrud. For some reason, he was unsuccessful in gaining election for another term. He returned to his family and his Houghton Angus ranch and died there on Jan. 24, 1969, of a heart condition. I still think of him and our good times together out on the campaign trail, especially whenever I pass that old blocky motel, still a haven for late-night travelers passing through Lake Preston.

South Dakota Governors
1. Arthur Calvin, Mellette, R, lawyer, Aberdeen, 1889-1893, died 5/25/1896
2. Charles H. Sheldon, R, farmer, Aberdeen, 1893-1897, died 10/14/1898
3. Andrew Ericson Lee, P, merchant, Vermillion, 1897-1901, died 3/19/34
4. Charles Nelson Herreid, R, lawyer, Leola, 1901-1905, died 7/6/28
5. Samuel Harrison Elrod, R, lawyer, Clark, 1905-1907, died 7/13/35
6. Coe Issac Crawford, R, lawyer, Huron, 1907-1909, died 4/25/44
7. Robert Scadden Vessey, R, real estate agent, Wessington Springs, 1909-1913, died 10/28/29
8. Frank M. Byrne, R, farmer, Faulkton, 1913-1917, died 12/25/27
9. Peter Norbeck, R, well driller, Redfield, 1917-1921, died 12/20/36
10. William H. McMaster, R, banker, Yankton, 1921-1925, died 9/14/68

11. Carl Gunderson, R, engineer, Mitchell, 1925-1927, died 2/16/33
12. William John Bulow, D, lawyer, Beresford, 1927-1931, died 2/26/60
13. Warren Everett Green, R, farmer, Hazel, 1931-1933, died 4/27/45
17. Tom Berry, D, rancher, Belvidere, 1933-1937, died 10/30/51
15. Leslie Jensen, R, lawyer, Hot Springs, 1937-1939, died 12/14/64
16. Harlan John Bushfield, R, lawyer, Miller, 1393-1943, died 9/27/48
17. Merrill Quentin Sharpe, R, lawyer, Ocoma, 1943-1947, died 1/22/62
18. George T. Mickelson, R, lawyer, Selby, 1947-1951, died 2/28/65
19. Sigard Anderson, R, lawyer, Webster, 1951-1955, died 12/02/90
20. Joseph J. Foss, R, businessman, Sioux Falls, 1955-1959, died 01/01/2003
21. Ralph E. Herseth, D, rancher, Houghton, 1959-1961, died 1/24/69
22. Archie M. Gubbrud, R, farmer, Alcester, 1961-1965, died 4/26/87
23. Nils Andreas Boe, R, lawyer, Sioux Falls, 1965-1969, died 7/30/92
24. Frank LeRoy Farrar, R, lawyer, Britton, 1969-1971, alive
25. Richard Francis Kneip, D, businessman, Salem, 1971-1978*, died 3/9/87.
26. Harvey Wollman, D, farmer, Hitchcock, 1978 (completed Kneip term)
27. William J. Janklow, R, lawyer, Brandon, 1979-1987
28. George Speaker Mickelson, R, lawyer, Brookings, 1987-1993**, died 4/19/93
29. Walter Dale Miller, R, rancher, New Underwood, 1993-1995
30. William J. Janklow, R, lawyer, Brandon, 1995-2003***
31. Michael Rounds, R, real estate, Pierre, 2003-

*Resigned July 24, 1978 to become ambassador to Singapore
**Died in a plane crash in Iowa, April 19, 1993
***Prevented from seeking governorship for a third term, he successfully ran for the open U. S. House of Representatives seat, defeating Democrat Stephanie Herseth, the granddaugher of former Gov. Ralph Herseth
D-Democrat   R-Republican   P-Populist

Dakota Wind and Food For Peace

The photograph above, taken on a windy day in 1960, has historic significance.

It was taken during the National Plowing Contest on the Ode Farm near Sioux Falls. Then-presidential candidate John Kennedy, at far left, seated next to then-Representative George McGovern, was minutes away from speaking to the large crowd of mostly farmers.

A brisk Dakota wind was skittering along (note Gov. Ralph Herseth, out on the campaign for a second term, in his light overcoat, third from right). As George McGovern recalls, Kennedy had a difficult time giving his speech because the wind had blown the pages of his comments around and they were hurriedly gathered up, but in the wrong order.

Later that day, on the way to another campaign speech in Mitchell, Kennedy remarked to McGovern that he didn't feel his comments at the plowing contest went well. McGovern, at a lecture at South Dakota State University in April 2003, recalled that day and that ride, and said he agreed with Kennedy that the speech had not been good.

As McGovern remembered, Kennedy then asked for McGovern's advice on what he might talk about at the upcoming Mitchell event. It was the chance McGovern had been waiting for. He suggested Kennedy tie this country's enviable ability to produce food, and the surpluses that then existed, into a discussion on how that bounty could help in the quest for world peace.

Kennedy's speech in Mitchell did suggest that the productivity of the farmer be applied as an instrument of change in the world to feed the hungry and lift up the oppressed. The speech was well received by farmers, always eager to find new markets for their crops.

In the election that fall, Kennedy was successful in his quest for the presidency, but both McGovern, who was running for the U.S. Senate, and Herseth, seeking a second term as governor, were unsuccessful.

Shortly after President Kennedy came to office, he recalled the trip from Sioux Falls to Mitchell and his speech at Mitchell. He appointed George McGovern as the first director of a new Food for Peace program.

So in a small way perhaps, the Dakota wind may have been the genesis of the Food for Peace program. Had Kennedy's written speech not gotten jumbled because of the winds out on the Ode Farm that day, he might not have gotten the Food for Peace idea from George McGovern as the two rode on to Mitchell.

TUCK'S POST CARD

CARTE POSTALE.

POSTKARTE.

(FOR ADDRESS ONLY.)

Hi-We had our Gala Days
celebration again last weekend. Big crowd. Did Jeb get
hog house shingled yet?
Come see us!
Carol

Dorothy Jamison
RR 3, Box 49
H_____, MN

GALA DAY AT WHITE St

Chapter 8

Last Dance Hall

One of the last of South Dakota's old time dance pavilions is still standing, having successfully fought off all that fox trotters, two steppers, and Mother Nature could throw at it for over eighty years.

It is believed to be the oldest of its kind in eastern South Dakota still in usable condition. "The Garden," as it is called, is located next to the baseball field in a beautiful, broad park along the banks of the Big Sioux River about a half-mile east of Flandreau. The first dance held in the hall in the 1920s had an oriental theme, and the hall became known as the Japanese Gardens.

During WW II, when America fought a bitter war with the Japanese, the name was changed out of patriotic choice to simply the Flandreau Dance Pavilion. As memories of the war faded, the name reverted to Riverview Gardens. In the 1970s long after WW II, it was re-christened the Japanese Gardens.

Until the year 2000, dances were held regularly with music by such well-known bands as the Al Godfredsen and the Sammy Jensen bands up on the pavilion's small, spotlighted stage.

But Mary and Bart Rosheim of Flandreau, who organized and managed the dances on two Saturday nights a month, decided to retire

The famous Japanese Gardens dance hall located in the Flandreau City Park along the Big Sioux River just east of Flandreau. *Chuck Cecil Photo*

about two years ago. No one has stepped forward to take on the job. Now, some wedding dances and other celebration dances that may be tied to some city-wide event are held at the Japanese Gardens from time to time, but most days during the dance season, there are no happy sounds of music wafting out from the pavilion across the spacious, tree-lined park.

The pavilion was built in 1919. During the heyday of dance halls sixty and seventy years ago, this area was dotted with popular dancing spots. Among them were the Showboat at Lake Benton, MN, the Arkota in Sioux Falls, the Dell Rapids Dance Hall, the Madison Dance Hall on the shores of Lake Madison, and others.

Fire, financing, and a change in musical tastes and dance steps meant the end of most of the pavilions. But the Japanese Gardens, perhaps because of its affiliation with the City of Flandreau, survived.

Nothing much has changed over the years under the hall's large roof. It still has some of the same magical ambiance as it did when the likes of Eddie Skeets, Al Hesse, and Lawrence Welk stopped by to play into the wee hours every Saturday night along the Big Sioux River.

The old, wooden, straight-backed booths are still there. Large wood window covers can be raised on warm summer nights to let the cool breezes flow in through screened windows. A homemade reflecting ball on the ceiling in the middle of the floor is still there, throwing out a darting array of light reflections, although the motor gave out a few years ago and it stopped rotating long before the dancing stopped.

Early-day developers in Flandreau named it the Japanese Gardens because it sounded slightly exotic and it offered opportunities for inexpensive decorative themes, with plenty of paper lanterns and crepe paper streamers the ladies would prepare with scissors and flour and water paste.

The builders also wanted a rotating, reflecting ball just like the one then the talk of the dance circuit that hung from the ceiling of the Roof Garden ballroom in Okoboji, IA. But when they checked on what a reflecting ball like the one at Okoboji would cost, they swallowed hard and decided to look for alternatives.

They inflated an old basketball bladder to about twice its size, slapped on layers of plaster of paris, and before the plaster dried, stuck on tiny round mirrors, possibly from empty rouge and powder cases donated by women of the community.

That reflecting ball is still hanging from the ceiling of the Japanese Gardens, giving the place a little inexpensive class just as good as the old Okoboji ball. Another store-bought ball is now suspended from the ceiling.

At some point in time, the City of Flandreau assumed ownership of the Japanese Gardens, and through the years, city officials have taken

Couples trip the light fantastic on the Japanese Gardens maple dance floor in the old pavilion still standing and in use in Flandreau's city park. The reflecting ball hanging from the ceiling at left was made in the 1920s by slathering plaster of paris on the blown up bladder of a basketball, then embedding small, round mirrors in it. *Chuck Cecil Photo*

pride in its stewardship. They have been willing to invest in maintenance and in improvements, and city employees have kept the hall in very good shape. In 1969, after a Big Sioux River flood nearly floated the Gardens away, the city installed a new maple floor to replace the original, water-ruined floor.

The first band ever to play at the Japanese Gardens after it opened in the late summer of 1919 was Mike's Imperial Orchestra of Pipestone. On July 18, 1928, the pavilion gained fame and more notoriety when it featured the Lawrence Welk band. Welk was said to be so impressed with the Flandreau pavilion that he returned time and time again during the '20s and '30s.

Once, the hall was used as a roller skating rink, but this didn't set well with the ballroom dancers in the community who loved tripping the light fantastic on the smooth, danceable maple floor. The skating soon stopped.

Until the Roshiems retired from planning and promoting the dances and worrying about all of the other problems of dance hall management in 2000, from seventy-five to one hundred couples were regular customers. But with the old dancers slowing down and retreating to their easy chairs on Saturday nights, the crowds were no longer sufficient to pay for the band and the other expenses.

Now, the old, venerable dance hall is empty and silent most nights. But the city has kept it in excellent condition, and it could be ready to spring back to action on a moment's notice.

It stands as a silent reminder of those less complicated days when the waltz and the two-step were the rage across South Dakota.

April Postcards

April 2, 1901: The Centerville City Council passed an ordinance today prohibiting marble playing on Broadway and Main.

April 4, 1977: Basketball teams from South Dakota State University and the University of South Dakota departed today to play the Cuba National Team. They lost the game.

April 4, 1889: Winds clocked at fifty miles an hour fanned a prairie fire approaching the community of Mt. Vernon from the northwest about 11 a.m. today. When it had passed through town, fifty-three of fifty-seven major structures were destroyed. To save postal records, the postmaster's daughters buried them along the railroad track. The fire burned over the spot, but the records were saved.

April 7, 1875: The Army expelled the Gordon-Russell Party from the Gordon Stockade in the southern Black Hills and stopped the party's mining operations near the present site of Custer.

April 7, 1805: Lewis and Clark began their historic journey from St. Louis.

April 7, 1960: Midland's new school was completed today. Heating was augmented by tapping into a nearby geothermal well.

April 8, 1862: The governor ordered twenty men of the Dakota Cavalry, with bayonets fixed, into the House of Representatives at Yankton "to preserve order, make arrests if necessary and protect the House in the peaceful performance of its duties."

April 8, 1953: Mobridge promoters removed the remains of Sitting Bull, Sioux medicine man, from his grave at Ft. Yates, ND, and buried them in a grave west of Mobridge. It is ten feet deep and covered with twenty tons of concrete. Sitting Bull was killed Dec. 15, 1890, near Mobridge.

April 9, 1952: Mrs. Herman Kaiser of Millboro, who hung her wash out to dry on Jan. 21, saw that wash for the first time two and one-half months later. The January blizzard of 1952 had covered it in a snowdrift.

April 10, 1860: George and Mary Stickney arrived on their homestead in Union County. Mary was the first white woman to settle in Dakota Territory.

April 10, 1949: An explosion demolished St. Mary's Catholic Church in Marion today during Palm Sunday services, killing seven and injuring sixty of the seventy-five worshippers.

April 10, 1883: The Sun Dance and other selected Sioux customs and religious ceremonies and practices were forbidden by an order signed today by the Secretary of the Interior in Washington.

April 11, 1879: Yankton State Hospital opened its doors, and seventeen men and women who had been in similar hospitals in Minnesota and Nebraska were admitted.

April 11, 1877: The Northwestern Express and Transportation Company started its stage line today between Bismarck and Deadwood with three coaches a week running both ways. The 211-mile trip took thirty-six hours and cost $23.

April 12, 1888: Sarah Campbell, aka Aunt Sally, died in Galena today. She was the first African American female in the Black Hills, serving as a cook for Gen. George Custer when he reconnoitered the hills in 1874. She is buried on Vinegar Hill above Galena.

April 14, 1912: Dan Grunstead of Miller, returning for a visit to his native Norway, was one of 1,503 people who died after the sinking of the White Star Line's Titanic in the Atlantic Ocean.

April 15, 1900: Henry Heintz, Elkton postmaster who invented and built an airship, tested the machine today in Aurora. The *Argus Leader* reported the flight a "flat failure."

April 15, 1892: Ft. Sisseton cannons were fired today signaling the opening of surplus Indian land on the Sisseton-Wahpeton Reservation for homesteading. The cannon is now one of several used for decorative purposes on the grounds of the Hughes County Courthouse in Pierre.

This historic Ft. Sisseton cannon is now one of several gracing the Hughes County Courthouse grounds. *Chuck Cecil Photo*

April 16, 1917: The Draper Town Board voted today to fill the hole that was dug in September of 1916 for a fire to heat air for a balloon ascension as part of the town's Labor Day celebration.

April 17, 1931: The worst dust storm to date obscured the sun in eastern South Dakota, billowing across part of the state. The frequent dust storms were called Black Rollers.

April 17, 1884: The steamboat *Nettie Baldwin* journeyed up the James River from Columbia, SD, to LeMoure, ND. The 65x18-foot craft was built in 1881. It was one of the steamboats that sailed the James until 1914.

April 17, 1886: A prairie fire took the life of Guri Dalager and badly burned his daughter Betsy near Grenville today. Betsy saved her life by jumping into the farm's well.

April 18, 1881: In an unusual atmospheric condition, residents of Twin Brooks awakened at 5:30 a.m. to see in the sky a reflection of the city of Milbank about a mile away. In nearby Ortonville, MN, residents saw trees with distinct branches showing, reflected from the Dakota Hills west of Twin Brooks. The rare phenomena lasted about ten minutes.

April 18, 1885: Jack Bell's body was found hanging from a ladder leaning against the Hughes County Courthouse flagpole in Pierre today. He had been lynched by a group from nearby Harold.

April 19, 1866: Samuel J. Brown rode 120 miles in a blizzard to correct an erroneous report of hostile Indians in the Sisseton area, thereby avoiding a possible catastrophe as troopers at Ft. Sisseton were preparing to pursue the peaceful band.

April 19, 1993: Gov. George S. Mickelson of Brookings and seven others were killed today when the state plane they were in crashed at 4 p.m. nine miles southwest of Dubuque, IA.

April 20, 1899: Peter C. Shannon, chief justice of the Territorial Supreme Court, was killed today in a horse runaway accident in San Diego, CA.

Former Gov. George S. Mickelson

April 23, 1884: Jim "Death Valley" Smith was born today in Deadwood. He would sign with the Chicago White Sox in 1909 and pitch nine seasons, amassing a 111-113 record, including one twenty-game season.

April 24, 1873: Gen. George Custer, eight-hundred men of the 7th Cavalry, seven hundred horses, and two hundred mules arrived in Yankton enroute to Ft. Abraham Lincoln near Bismarck. A surprise, two-day blizzard forced Custer's troopers and animals to shelter in Yankton homes and barns.

April 24, 1886: A proclamation by Gov. Gilbert A. Pierce ordered Arbor Day to be observed for the first time in Dakota Territory.

April 26, 1878: Deadwood was platted in Deadwood Gulch today. Lumber sawed by hand there sold for $150 per thousand board feet.

April 26, 1920: Thomas VanDerVort Garlock died today at his home in Custer where he had lived since arriving in Dakota Territory from New York in 1884. He is credited with inventing the plunger-type sprayer such as is used in the fly sprayer.

April 26, 1911: The Kirkham stage bound for White Owl overturned on a hill near the Fish Ranch today, and one passenger suffered a broken collar bone and numerous bruises. Too late, the stage driver discovered there were no brakes, and the four horses got out of control going down a hill near the ranch.

April 27, 1984: A circus traveling west on Interstate 90 was caught in a snow storm and stranded in Kadoka. Elephants and other circus animals were housed in warm filling stations.

April 28, 1899: A brush fire started by H. C. McNary on his farm six miles north of Kimball in Waldo Township got out of control and swept over fifty thousand acres in Bruce County plus thousands more acres in Buffalo, Jerauld, Aurora, and Davison counties.

April 28, 1902: Fire destroyed the half-block square Grain Palace in Aberdeen today. It was built in 1893 and could seat four thousand.

April 28, 1910: Triplets were born today to Mr. and Mrs. Judson Mallory, who ranched south of Vale. The children were named Elsie, Vera, and Hazel.

April 29, 1949: Four former governors plus current Governor George Mickleson were present today to dedicate Governor's Grove northeast of Capitol Lake. A tree from each county is planted in the grove, and a stone from each county is cemented into a decorative arch.

April 29, 1882: Mitchell city officials today ordered Street Commissioner F. H. Hamilton to stop filling potholes with manure, saying it was a very temporary solution to a permanent problem.

April 30, 1803: President Thomas Jefferson and Napoleon sealed the deal to allow the U.S. to buy what is known as the Louisiana Purchase for $11,250,000. That figures to about three cents an acre. With interest, the cost was $27,267,622.

POST CARD

GILBERT

Folks and all:

Kate took us to court house
today to watch the big wheels
turn...slowly. Jimmy broke his
arm, fell from tree. OK now.
Peg with love

PS–Grandpa drinks his coffee
from a saucer. Yuk!

Mr. and Mrs. Lester Durand
R.R. 3. Box #21

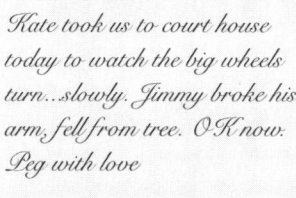

Chapter 9

Coffee Code of Ethics

Our coffee group has taken a page from the Brookings City Council. We're revising our ages-old Code of Ethics, too.

City leaders at one time wanted to require unpaid, loyal volunteer members of the city's various boards and commissions to sign a written agreement that they would not conduct city business in an unethical or dishonest fashion.

Has it been a problem in the past?

Not since the last Ice Age.

But it sounded like a good idea, so being a progressive bunch, our coffee group has decided to do the same.

The original coffee group code was written in longhand in number two pencil lead by the late Irvin Dybdahl, a local car dealer in the mid-twentieth century. He scribbled it out on a coffee-stained napkin on the table in the back of the old Staley's Café, which is now a Chinese restaurant. The napkin code from way back was becoming fragile and brittle, which incidentally, pretty well describes some of our current coffee members who bought cars from Irv.

Our new document will take into account the changing times and will mirror to some degree the controversial code city leaders pushed until citizens shoved back. I'm not sure what ever became of the city's order to volunteers, but our coffee group decided to make the changes quickly before we forgot about it.

We decided not to be as Draconian as city leaders. At least I think they are Draconian. I haven't seen their code, but some of my friends say that volunteers who do not sign the thing will be shot at sunrise.

I hardly believe that.

We're going to make our delinquents sit for a week's worth of daily meetings in the chair directly under the café's hard-working air conditioning vent.

Our coffee group has a glorious history in Brookings. It was started in the late 1940s after the war. In fact, some of the original members still attend the 10 a.m. weekday sessions.

So far we've pretty much agreed upon a new pledge in our preamble. Because of recent California court rulings and what seems to be a national project of the American Civil Liberties Union (ACLU), we've removed the ending phrase: "So Help Me God." As a substitute we've jotted down "if the sun comes up and the creek don't rise." We hope that will meet with the ACLU's approval.

In the paragraph establishing a dress code, we'll strike the requirement that every member must have on at least one clothing item made of polyester which covers all but head and feet, and add a requirement that members wear one item of golf clothing, even during the winter. Golf has of course ended, but many of our members still talk of the shot that might have been.

In view of the Monica Lewinsky/Bill Clinton scandal, we're substituting the word "footwear" in the paragraph that refers to "thongs" so there can be no misunderstanding.

In the clause on educational requirements of members, we're deleting the word "Mensa" and in its place, substituting "eighth grade education or its equivalency." Incidentally, we have appointed a sub-committee to search out the meaning of the word "Mensa" and to report back in six months.

We decided to appoint the committee after several members insisted "Mensa" was a car model from the late 1940s or early 1950s.

As a special membership requirement we are removing the term "know-it-all," and adding the more academic-sounding and accurate requirement that members be "experts on everything under the sun."

In the paragraph that sets meeting time limits, we considered shortening the one-hour sessions because some of the members, particularly those who claimed to be charter members, were beginning to nod off at about the forty-five-minute mark. One of the charter members also said that the longer meetings were expensive for him, since in the winter he leaves his car's motor running through the coffee break. I believe he drives a 1949 Mensa.

To comply with the Environmental Protection Agency and newly-enacted state laws, we've inserted a "no cigarette smoking" amendment into our code. Pipes and cigars will still be allowed at the down-wind end of the table, which is also closer to the back door in case any of the EPA police raid the joint.

On another coffee group matter, we've been researching whether cream substitutes are safe for members to use. Some members suspect that there are steroids in the fake cream's formula. We have observed that members who use cream substitutes have full heads of hair and seem to be able to get up from their chairs at the end of our sessions without either grunting, becoming exceptionally light headed, or having to sink back in the chair a few times to build momentum for one final try.

We don't know if it's the fake cream or not, but we certainly want to find out.

POST CARD

Uncle Rex caught a chicken
and Aunt Rose cooked it.
Good. Will start for home
tomorow a.m.
Love and kisses
Robert

Genevieve, Geo. Smith
RR 4, Box 19

Chapter 10

Chicken Sexers
and Buffalo Wings

I was wrong.

Here I've spent my life believing that the Japanese had a corner on the chicken sexing market only to find out that with a little training, just about anyone can do it.

All they have to do is wing it, so to speak. Let me explain.

The Japanese, with perhaps a brief hiatus during WW II, were until then the world's foremost chicken sexers. Teams from the Land of the Rising Sun toured the little towns of the Midwest and wherever else baby chicks were hatched in this country. They made a pretty penny sorting the little chicks by their gender. The future hens went into one box, and future roosters were tossed unceremoniously into another.

How the Japanese experts figured out a chick's sex has always been their well-kept secret. But however they managed it, they could sex chickens faster than hogs on ice. I've never studied the methods in too much detail because it simply was not possible. The process was over very quickly. All I remember about the process carried out over a couple of days down at the farmers coop was that there was a flurry of hands and flapping wings and sawdust and little chicken feathers flying off in all directions. And that was it.

The chickens peeped and squeaked as you might do if someone turned you upside down and started parting your chicken feathers to either throw you to the left or right, depending on what they found down there.

I can't be entirely certain, but I think the Japanese chicken sexer methodology involved two of the five senses. So for thousands of years, chickens were deposited in appropriate boxes using the Japanese system which had an accuracy rate of something like ninety-nine percent.

The Japanese Method was it, as sure as the laws of physics.

But wait!

It came to my complete surprise that the Japanese method is now kaput. I learned that the day I attended a meeting in Flandreau to update the membership on the progress of the Dakota Layers Cooperative egg plant. The idea was to provide a home for upwards of three-quarters of a million laying hens in huge fifty by five hundred foot-long chicken houses sprawled out on an acreage in northern Moody County west of Ward and north of Flandreau.

The chicken grower from Sioux Rapids, Iowa, who would hatch the eggs and grow the hens for about three months before having them trucked to the Moody County chicken houses, told of the trials and tribulations of turning out nearly a million baby chicks for sale to egg factories.

First of all, chickens are a sickly lot and easy prey for such things as chicken pox and bronchitis. Like sheep, they're liable to just up and die on you for no known reason whatsoever.

Aside from just keeping the chicks alive and healthy, it is up to the hatchery owner to insure that when sending out laying hens by the hundreds of thousands, the laying hens are in fact laying hens. That's why the profession of chicken sexing started, and as I've mentioned, it was dominated for centuries by skilled Japanese sexers.

But all that has changed. Hatcheries now use ordinary people like you and me. A couple of hours of training and we, too, could commence to sort chickens like sixty. The sex of the little, inconsequential, innocent baby chicks can be determined, it has been discovered, by the shape of its wing feathers. Males have more geometrically pleasing wing feather patterns. Unfortunately for the girl chicks, but fortunately for the chicken sexers, female baby chicks' feathers resemble a bad hair day.

A good chicken sexer using the wing ID method can zing along at a sexing speed of 1,500 chicks an hour.

So what happens to those unfortunate chicks with the nice-looking wings judged to be future roosters? I'm not sure, but I have this theory that they are sent out to Custer State Park and packed in a liberal dose of dried ice.

There, these beautiful rooster wings are surgically removed with a hedge trimmer and implanted in a small incision in the shoulders of the Custer State Park buffalo.

After a year or so, the wings are again clipped off and sold to a wholesaler who will ship them to fast food restaurants that cater to teenagers and the young at heart. The wings find their way onto the menus but aren't called chicken wings.

That's because chicken wings have been the part of the chicken that for thousands of years man has tried to avoid eating. The other part is called the Pope's Nose, which is the little flap at the back of the chicken which gives it a modicum of privacy. I suspect the Pope's Nose becomes something like a chicken nugget at the fast food stores.

There has always been a glut of chicken wings on the market. If there was a Spam for chicken parts as there is for unmentionable beef parts, the wings would be the main ingredients.

Happily, food specialists have found a way to rid the planet of its overabundance of chicken wings. They are listed on menus as Buffalo Wings, and served with a sauce that dilutes the taste of the ubiquitous wing of chicken.

I'm told that Buffalo wings (i.e. chicken wings) are an invention of a restaurant in Buffalo, NY, where a sauce was concocted to make the chicken wing more palatable. But I'm sticking with the Custer State Park theory.

 May Postcards

May 1, 1910: The South Dakota Capitol building was completed today.

May 1, 1893: President Grover Cleveland opened the Chicago World's Fair and as part of the event, the Forest City (SD) Man was on display. It later was found to be a hoax. This fabrication of an ancient human was ostensibly found near the Little Cheyenne River near Forest City. It was a fake created by Forest City butcher William Sutton and a Redfield physician. They were helped by William Horn, a lime burner, and James Sutton. A body cast was made in Redfield of James Sutton. A human skeleton of unknown origin was then placed in the cast, which was then filled with cement. The creation was aged and painted. Horn then reported he had found the petrified man in his search for limestone and the public bought it, for a time.

May 2, 1852: Martha Cannary, aka Calamity Jane, was born today in Princeton, NJ.

May 3, 1883: Laura Ingalls of DeSmet, who would later write *Little House on the Prairie* and other books about pioneer days, was a bridesmaid at the wedding of Jennie May Ross, a Kingsbury County teacher, and Walter W. Wheat of DeSmet.

May 3, 1920: A wedding was held today in Wind Cave, because, it is said, the bride had promised her mother that she would marry no man on the face of the earth. Mr. and Mrs. H. C. Magorian of Auburn, CA, revisited their wedding site in June 1958 while on a trip to South Dakota.

May 3, 1931: Gypsy Oil Co. of Tulsa, OK, started drilling near Wall today. A celebration sponsored by the Wall Commercial Club was held to celebrate the venture. It was to be Wall's salvation. It was reported that ten thousand people showed up. At six thousand feet, the dry well was closed and the drilling company returned to Oklahoma. Later, Wall Drug Store hit upon the idea of stimulating economic development by giving away free ice water to passing motorists.

May 4, 1877: Throughout the area, a Prayer Day was held to ask devine guidance and relief from a grasshopper plague.

May 4, 1891: Tripp city officials passed a motion today instructing the marshal to notify the butchers in town to start slaughtering animals one-half mile beyond the city limits, rather than in town.

May 4, 1876: William Cogan was killed today by Indians at the site that is now the St. Patrick's interchange in Rapid City. He had left for Rapid City from his home in Tyndall when he met his death just outside the city.

May 6, 1877: Chief Crazy Horse surrendered today at Ft. Robinson, NB.

May 7, 1852: Charlie (Raspberry) Brown was born today in Binghampton, NY. He became a well-known miner at Carbonate, now a ghost town near Lead. He arrived in the Black Hills in 1875 and died near Deadwood in April 1939. He was called Raspberry because when not mining, he made a slim living picking and selling raspberries to local housewives and miners.

May 7, 1876: General George Custer and the 7th Cavalry left Ft. Abraham Lincoln today headed for the Little Big Horn.

May 9, 1934: A black blizzard of dust rolled into Watertown today at 3 p.m., turning day into night.

May 11, 1881: The Mitchell pesthouse, for people with contagious diseases to stay in until cured, was assigned to receive deceased small pox victims until they could be buried.

May 11, 1907: The railroad reached Philip at about 10 a.m. today.

May 11, 1930: Richard Clark, aka Deadwood Dick, was buried at sunset today in Mt. Moriah cemetery in Deadwood.

May 12, 1901: The first baseball game ever played in Selby took place today with the home team winning over Java 37-4.

May 12, 1898: The first circus ever to perform in Sioux Falls was brought to town by the local owners, the Buchanan Brothers, who used local talent, then went on the road until bankruptcy stalled the show in Pipestone, MN, just thirty days later.

May 13, 1887: The *Hot Springs Star* reported today that a man from "Rio Janero, Brazil" was visiting in the city to use the hot springs there.

May 13, 1843: John J. Aubudon, famous naturalist, entered what is now South Dakota today. He traveled up the Missouri River, leaving the state June 5, just twenty-two days after entering. While in the state, he observed and identified sixty-one different birds.

May 13, 1916: Oscar Howe, renowned Indian artist, was born today on the Crow Creek Agency.

May 13, 1920: The first air mail service arrived in Belle Fourche from Missoula, MT, today aboard a Norwest Aircraft Corp. plane out of Newell, SD, piloted by H. H. Rowe.

May 14, 1925: Singer Patrice Muncel, who lived as a young girl in Centerville, was born today in Spokane, WA.

May 15, 1856: L. Frank Baum, the author who in 1902 wrote the classic *Wizard of Oz* and who lived in Aberdeen in the late 1880s and early 1890s, was born today at Chittenango, NY.

May 15, 1915: J. W. Parmley of Ipswich, president of the Yellowstone Trail Association promoting travel on proscribed routes, arrived in Ortonville fifteen minutes behind schedule because of muddy roads the Studebaker Six he was driving encountered between Twin Brooks and Marvin. He became the first person to travel by auto across the state, from Lemmon to Ortonville.

May 15, 1922: A Hudson farmer, before selling his eggs today for 18 cents a dozen, wrote his name and address on one of the eggs. A year later, in May 1923, he heard from a man in eastern Massachuesetts who said he had paid 42 cents a dozen for the Hudson eggs and found the message on one of them.

May 16, 1919: Tipperary Day, honoring a fourteen-year-old bucking horse by the same name, was held today in Camp Crook. Over two thousand people showed up to help honor the horse that cowboys said "couldn't be rode."

May 17, 1915: Aberdeen leaders discussed the so-called "dinner ordinance" that mandated wives be home each day not later than 11:30 a.m. and 5:30 p.m. The city council later learned the proposed ordinance was introduced in jest.

May 18, 1932: Four robbers took $21,000 from the Ipswich Bank. One bank employee was injured by gunshot, and Chester Doolittle, the cashier, was kidnapped. The bandits were later caught and sentenced to twenty years in the penitentiary. Doolittle survived the ordeal.

May 19, 1904: The notorious character Jack Sully, former Charles Mix County Sheriff who won the election 61-1 at a time when only fifty-five people lived in the entire county, died of a gunshot wound today when he refused to give himself up to answer cattle rustling charges.

May 19, 1941: The RJB riverboat, loaded with 71,400 board feet of cottonwood logs enroute to Yankton where they were to become egg crates, passed DeGray below Pierre, the last commercial haul on the river above Yankton.

May 20, 1870: Joe Parson of rural Darlington (now Gann Valley) traded his horse for a tame buffalo and the Parson Brothers Circus was born. In 1881 he hired a juggler for $9 a week named Al Ringling, who later bought the circus and started one with his brother.

May 20, 1916: The 4th South Dakota National Guard was called into federal service today and sent to the Mexican border.

May 21, 1883: William Combellick, who would invent and manufacture the Combellick Hog Waterer, arrived to take up a home in Gettysburg.

May 21, 1962: A tornado skipped across Douglas County today damaging forty-two rural homes and destroying fifty-eight barns, forty-five grain storage buildings, and 129 other buildings. Miraculously, no one was injured.

May 21, 1881: E. B. Adams, who would come up with the idea of Hot Springs hosting the annual Miss South Dakota Pageant, was born today.

May 22, 1877: Fr. John Lonergan, who had only recently arrived in the Black Hills from Omaha, celebrated the first mass in the Black Hills in a Deadwood carpenter's shop.

May 21, 1923: Clay B. Platner of Crow Township, Jerauld County, became ill while staying in the Oliver Hotel in Wessington Springs today. Near death, with his physician and the hotel proprietor at his bedside, he dictated this last will and testament: "She gets everything-Dora." It was the shortest legal will ever in South Dakota.

May 25, 1918: Ten-year-old Harold France and his sister Geraldine, both of Burke, were caught in a sudden hail storm in an open field while herding cattle. The girl made it to safety, but Harold, thinking his sister was lost in the storm, remained in the open to look for her. When found alive after the storm, he was covered with bruises, his clothing was blood-soaked, and stitches were required to close his scalp wounds.

May 25, 1902: The government had ordered cattlemen to move their herds from the free range of the Rosebud Sioux Reservation, and today, sixty cowboys launched the famous "last roundup" in South Dakota to gather the cattle in compliance. The roundup would last until July 4.

May 27, 1899: Charles Peterson and six Peterson children ages three to fourteen were killed today in a tornado that struck near Academy. Mrs. Peterson and two other children survived.

May 27, 1918: At a special session of the Legislature, with WW I continuing in Europe, lawmakers banned the use of the German language in church services or at public or semi-public meetings.

May 28, 1931: Seven inches of rain fell in Watertown in two hours today, but in nearby Castlewood, no rain fell at all.

May 29, 1960: Ground was broken today for the Big Bend Dam near the site of old Ft. Thompson south of Highmore.

May 30, 1910: The first monument in South Dakota honoring the Grand Army of the Republic was dedicated today in Milbank. Costing $1,200, it was the first of many honoring Civil War veterans to be placed on courthouse grounds in the state.

POST CARD

UNITED STATES POSTAGE 1 CENT

Dear Mother and Dad
got here yesterday noon.
Went shopping in big store
today. Didn't buy any-
thing, just looked. They
had everything and then
some. Second floor was
clothes and stuff. Love and
kisses.   Amanda

Mr. and Mrs. David Budd
RR 3, Box 7

Chapter 11

They Have Everything

If you can't find what you want at Myron and Nila Ondricek's store in Iroquois, you probably didn't need it in the first place.

Their unusual New to You emporium is jammed with more antiques, collectibles, and other of society's castaway flotsam and jetsam than you can shake a stick at. And it wouldn't be a surprise to me if they also had some old sticks for sale there, too.

The items line the aisles, hang from the walls, teeter atop and balance beneath shelves and cases, sit on precarious perches, and spill out into an adjoining building.

You walk at your own risk.

The Huron couple drives eighteen miles east on Highway 14 every day but Sunday to open their unique emporium of organized randomness. Hours are from 2 to 5 p.m. There are three floors of what can best be described as "stuff," everything from dried-out horse hames, tiny tins of army gun oil, bottles of Arrowhead Mills olive oil in a colorful apothecary display, fire hoses, wicker chairs, celluloid beauty tools, fruit jars, horns, limp-stringed guitars, and auto magnetos, to name a few.

The Ondriceks believe their chaotic assemblage contains the largest inventory of any business of its kind in eastern South Dakota or western Minnesota. They are probably right. Even if they aren't, who's going to challenge them?

They have no idea of the number of items they have hauled into the drafty one-hundred-year-old structure during their eighteen years in this community of three hundred. They picked Iroquois for their store

The New To You store may have the state's largest selection of a good share of everything under the sun. *Chuck Cecil Photo* because "the price was right," says Myron. Buildings in their hometown of Huron were too expensive to rent or buy.

In reporting to accountants and tax collectors about their copious inventory, they make only an educated guess. "We try to figure out what's along one wall and then multiply," says Nila, who was born near Iroquois. "If they want to come out and count it to make sure we're right, they're welcome to it."

Every square inch of space in the building and one attached to the rear of the twenty-eight by sixty-five-foot brick structure is occupied by collections of one thing or another. On a meandering tour of the premises one cold winter day, strolling past tinkling old pop and beer bottles awakened by the footsteps on swaying floorboards, Myron points out worn wooden boxes filled with smaller wooden boxes in the dimly-lit recesses near the back of the store. "Those are flue dampers," he says, his breath rolling out in a white cloud in the unheated corner.

A retired mechanic, Myron was born in Highmore. At times, scrunching sideways to detour past items that have spilled out into the aisle, he seems surprised to find something he'd forgotten he bought at auction years ago. He points with proprietary pride at society's knicks and knacks packed in narrow passageways in the former funeral home and hardware store.

"See here," he points out, "this is the elevator we used to haul the stuff down in the basement or upstairs with." He explains that the elevator has been converted to storage space to help house their copious

Myron and Nila Ondricek, at right, bargain with antique collector Maynard Hahn of Howard, left, in their unusual New to You store in Iroquois on Highway 14 east of Huron. The Ondriceks have filled three stories and a large storeroom with antiques, collectibles, and unusual, hard-to-find items. *Chuck Cecil Photo*

collection. For the past fifty years they've been "dabbling and piddling in antiques," as Nila puts it.

The store's front door activates a tinkling bell as Maynard Hahn, 70, of Howard, walks in out of the cold. He's been collecting toys and tokens and souvenirs for forty years and stops by the New to You store several times a year. "This little old store is a good place to pick up commemorative things," he says. "In fact, you can just about find anything here."

On this day, he fingers a commemorative coin with a price tag of $22.50. Jokingly feigning bad eyesight, he repeats the price at $2.50 to the guffaws of Myron and Nila. After some friendly bargaining, the old friends settle on a reduced price of $21 for the coin.

Nila's special interest in antiques includes glassware. Myron's is anything made of paper. "I like paper," he says.

Among his "paper" collection are old ice delivery coupons, operating manuals for motor vehicles long since retired and rusted, and advertising ink blotters. "But wait until you see our library," he says. The Ondriceks, neither of whom graduated from high school, have amassed a collection of books old and new that would put many small libraries to shame.

From a hidden recess in an old cupboard Myron digs around and pulls out a South Dakota Vehicle Registration card from Spink County. It's dated 1927 and lists James Manson of Redfield as the owner of a 1925 Model T 1925 Touring Ford.

They explain that to keep up with the changing interests of people who are into collectibles and antiques, they have to stay one step ahead. "For instance," says Myron, "it used to be round oak tables were popular, but now they want chrome kitchen tables with yellow tops."

Also high on the list of collectibles are the plastic toys given away by fast food hamburger chains. And the spindly-legged California raisin man featured in advertising years ago is also popular.

Iroquois no longer has a hardware store, so local customers drop by not only to purchase antiques, but also to buy bent nails and used screws and bolts for household repairs. Used electrical supplies are kept in the drawers of an old chicken brooder cabinet.

The Ondriceks also have regular customers from throughout South Dakota and in nearly every state. Nila recalls a visit several years ago by Hollywood officials preparing to film *Dances With Wolves* in western South Dakota. "They bought tin cups, cast iron kettles, and horse hobblers," she recalls. "We only have one horse hobbler left now," she says, picking up the soapstone object which was also used to heat beds in the days before central heating.

Perhaps their most unusual sale contributed to insuring that the DM&E Railroad ran through town on time. "A crew was putting in a new crossing down the street," Nila says. "They came in and said they ran out of railroad spikes and if we didn't have any, they would have to drive back to Huron to get some more."

She and Myron dug around the store and found some.

"They bought all eight and were able to finish the job," she says.

Myron has had a kidney transplant and Nila has had bypass heart surgery. That hasn't slowed them down. They plan to continue to keep their unusual store going as long as they're able. "We're not dealing with heavy stuff anymore because we just can't haul it around by ourselves," says Nila. But whatever it is they intend to stock in their unusual store in the future, it will most surely still be nearly "new to you."

POST CARD

Place the Stamp here
ONE CENT
For United States
...essions
...da and
...o
...NTS
...ign

Mother and Father
We went skating on the lake
today and watched men fish
for a car. Hard work—skating that is. (Joke)
Hiram

Mr. and Mrs. Ted Black
RR 3, Box 45

Chapter 12

Bobber Shock

There seems to be no end to new diseases that we must all worry and fret about. The latest malady is so new it isn't even covered by Blue Cross.

I'm talking, of course, of the disorder common mostly in the Midwest, and striking only the brave and hardy souls who fish through the ice.

I have reported this illness to the *New England Journal of Medicine* and just completed a long letter to our president urging him to instruct his Surgeon General to discontinue the use of billions of dollars for research on the study of the effects of eating chickens who have died of

This lone angler drills through the ice on Twin Lakes south of Arlington on Highway 81, preparing to drop his line and enter the ice fisherman's trance which can easily lead to bobber shock. *Chuck Cecil Photo*

boredom, and the research to learn what happens after a person becomes completely fatheaded.

Instead, I'm urging that this money be channeled into a detailed investigation of Bobber Shock.

Until we learn just what the president intends to do, I feel an obligation to warn all wives out there who may have husbands who for some reason or other enjoy freezing their keesters out on an ice-encased lake. They are in grave danger. My advice is to try to convince them to stay home.

Misery may love company, but not out on the ice. Put your husband in your deep freeze for an afternoon if you have to. There's probably more action there than out on the lake, anyway.

Wives need to know that more and more ice fishermen are having to be forcefully skidded off the frozen Dakota lakes laid out on their scoop shovels, stiff as a road-killed and sun-dried carp, or strapped to their pitifully built, homemade wooden toboggans.

Or if the shock is too far advanced. they may be stuffed unmercifully into their faithful five-gallon plastic buckets and carried off to the nearest pool hall for medical treatment. After extensive research, I have determined just how bobber shock affects the ice fisherman.

Normally, the candidate for this pestilence is prone to arrive at a lake before sun-up on a stormy weekend. Ice fishermen tend to fish alone, since their conversation on fishing day falls off dramatically and their vocabulary becomes limited. Unlike normal people who prefer to spend the day with warm, more lucid company, fishermen crave discomfort. They would just as soon be left alone in their own personal, lonely misery.

The ice fisherman has left home very early, as I've mentioned, having spent an hour packing gear into either his green plastic pickle bucket or his white plastic dry wall cement bucket.

This bucket business is something of a status symbol for ice fishermen. The number owned divides ice fishermen into castes. Just as the plains Indians with herds of horses were held in more esteem than warriors with just one or two horses, ice fishermen are judged by how many plastic buckets they own.

Bucket owners may spend hours grooming their "herd," mounting bottle holders or little places to hold their portable radios, attaching cushioned seats to the tops and carefully soaking off the "Gedney Non-Garlic" or "Alfredo's Best Sheet Rock Cement" labels stuck on the side.

Old Air Force veterans turned ice fishermen often paint numbers on the flanks of their beloved buckets, and also may add a name, such as "Oh, Mama" or "Patty Pike" or "Whoa Boy" or "Mudpuppy" or something racy and unprintable except on the ice, where language often deteriorates to the lowest common denominator.

Some ice fishermen have devised padded covers made of the "breast of fawn" fur for their buckets, which will serve as a chair seat for their weathered wazoos once they arrive at the aquatic killing grounds.

Items packed into the ubiquitous pickle bucket include a short fishing pole, a spare pole in the highly unlikely event a large fish comes along and steals the first one, and a piece of a car antennae in the very unlikely event another big fish comes along and torpedoes the spare pole.

There is also a tin can full of rusty teardrop fish hooks, a hunk of year old chislic believed to have been left in the crotch of a tree by the Lewis and Clark Expedition, several battle-damaged slip bobbers, a rusty pair of pliers to be used as a surgical instrument to remove rusty

While he is using the legal number of fish lines, this Sioux Falls fisherman has prepared several holes in Lake Campbell ice in search of just the right spot to catch elusive perch, walleye, and northerns. *Chuck Cecil Photo*

teardrop hooks snagged in the cold hands of the fisherman, a small radio held together with duct tape and permanently tuned to WNAX, a topographic map of the area, depth charts of the lakes, a pint of Blackberry Brandy in a plain paper sack (used for medicinal purposes), three greasy gloves with ragged cuffs and a dozen hooks snagged in them, a small jackknife so rusty it can't be opened, an autographed picture of outdoorsman Tony Dean (who has magically metamorphized into a political crony), a book of wet matches, and a Prince Albert tobacco can filled with moist mattress stuffing onto which cling a variety of maggots, fruit fly larva, wax worms, and goldenrod grubs.

When not on the ice, incidentally, this can of bait is stored under the fisherman's pillow. Old-time, veteran fishermen are said to carry bait inside their lower lip like a pinch of tobacco, which helps explain why old-time ice fishermen are known to be extremely grouchy and seldom open their mouths to visit.

Optional equipment includes a half-used roll of toilet paper, a flashlight held together with duct tape, some reading material, such as the operator's manual for a Ski-Doo snowmobile, and a metal ice skimmer (with edges curled from banging it against the plastic bucket to knock off ice accumulations). This skimmer usually still has the price tag on it and sports a soiled feed tag wired to the handle on which the fisherman's wife has written in large, red crayon: "Remember The Pump-Handle Rule-Keep This Out Of Your Mouth."

The sun is usually up by the time ice fishermen have arrived at the lake and have checked their depth charts and topographic maps to determine where the exact center of the lake is, since ice fishermen incorrectly assume that because the earth is spinning, fish will be centrifugally forced to the center of any large body of water.

After the ice hole is dug and the plastic bucket put into place, the ritual of preparing the fishing line begins. Ice fishermen attach little metal, snap-on depth finders to their coat pocket flaps and coat collars much the same as Marines attach hand grenades to belts looped over their shoulders. These little weighted objects are snapped onto a length of line and lowered into the lake to verify that the depth of the water is what their electronic depth finder says it is.

The lead depth finder is brought up and replaced on the pocket flap, a maggot or larva or whatever is attached to the rusted teardrop hook, the slip bobber is set for the right depth, and the long, cold, miserable, boring wait for a fish to come along begins. From time to time, stealth rattlesnakes are beaten back and brandy is consumed for snake bite protection. It isn't long before the fisherman enters a hypnotic state. All bodily functions slow down, including the ability to speak complete sentences.

Ice fishermen have been known to sit in this Valhallic haven atop their plastic buckets for hours, moving only to ward off rattler attacks or to turn the radio volume up when it's time for the farm market report. The rest of the time, perhaps twelve to fifteen hours at a stretch, the ice fisherman sits stoically and silently.

Seldom does the bobber ever move from the center of the hole in the ice. For over ninty-nine percent of the time out on a frozen lake, absolutely nothing moves, except the slow, nearly imperceptible, groaning journey of his breakfast of two cold Millers, three pounds of Santitas Tortilla Chips, and the pint of salsa now coursing along making white caps somewhere deep in his digestive tract. But sometimes, after hours of waiting in the numbing cold and watching the non-moving bobber for hours on end until his eyes itch, a slight breeze may waft across the quiet lake.

It catches the aerodynamically designed bobber, and the little float begins to migrate ever so slightly within the small, ice-framed fishing hole. When this happens, it has been found that in about fifteen percent of the cases, the fisherman actually believes the one fish in the lake that is awake is showing some interest in his hook, and the fisherman goes rapidly from his heavenly state into what is medically known as "Dumbfoundnessitis Norskedamus" or, as it has come to be called, Bobber Shock.

In Bobber Shock, eyes are set in a wide, surprised look, eyebrows are arched in very pronounced "U's," and gnarly hands grow purple from the death grip on the small pole. Beechnut-stained spittle highlights bearded chins.

If you should come upon what you assume to be a bobber-shocked fisherman out there on the ice, the Game, Fish and Parks Department recommends the following procedure:

1. Approach from the downwind side cautiously and quietly.

2. As gently as possible, lay him aside, put gear into his bucket (don't forget the Prince Albert bait can in his overalls breast pocket) and dump all this into the back of your pickup. This is not an illegal act if done on the ice, for there is an obscure paragraph in the U.S. Constitution which is known as the Law of The Ice. It states that the finder of abandoned or unattended gear can assume immediate ownership.

3. Sprinkle the anti-snake solution on the ice around the inert fisherman, pin a "Do Not Disturb" sign to his cap, and head for the pool hall. Chances are the bobber-shocked fisherman will not be missed until spring anyhow, so you may as well leave him there in his sublime trance for the remainder of winter.

POST CARD

Place the Stamp here
ONE CENT
United States
ssions and
TS
gn

Hello from North Pole!!!
Men fishing on ice so we went
to town. Alma and Bert had
picture taken at Haddoff's
Store. They look cold and
unhappy, don't they?
See you Wednesday if I get
home.
Druzelda

Minnie and Geo. Locker
R.R. 5, Box 2

AUTIE ALMA
AND
BERTHA MAE
DRESSED FOR
WINTER

Chapter 13

Pickle Buckets

We discussed in the last chapter on Bobber Shock the close association an ice fisherman has with his beloved collection of plastic pickle or sheet rock cement buckets. In this chapter we will explore in more detail the bucket and show a rare photograph of a typical herd of plastic pickle buckets grazing peacefully on the summer range during the off season.

As we have established, pickle buckets to the ice fisherman are extremely important in the conduct of the Hierarchy of the Ice. The more a fisherman's herd of buckets is trained and tamed and the larger his herd, the more respect an ice fisherman has among his peers. Pickle or sheet rock cement buckets on the ice denote fishing wisdom and wealth.

The owner of a large herd of plastic buckets out on the ice can expect amenities from others with less established herds. There'll be

A herd of pickle bucket breeding stock whiling away the summer on an Alpine-like meadow, putting on plastic fat for the coming winter ice fishing season. *Chuck Cecil Photo*

plenty of free deer jerky, an extra can of Old Mil, and maybe even a complimentary pint jar of some homemade salsa to help liven up an otherwise lonely, cold, miserable afternoon out on the ice.

The photograph shown on the previous page was obtained after hours of stalking the herd and finally approaching down wind close enough to record the habits of the buckets as they went about their daily routine on a high mountain meadow lush with buffalo and blue grass.

Scientifically, a herd of mostly white pickle buckets is known within the academic community as Gringo Rearuppitus Wazooities. The photograph shows that the owner of the herd has not only developed a fine stock of useful plastic pickle buckets, but also has a healthy-looking crop of yearlings, called "pails," and a recently born "dish" which you can see in the lower left hand corner. The well-fed bucket at lower right has a slight greenish sheen, and it, along with the other off-colored buckets in this herd, will probably never see duty on the ice. They will be culled from the herd and sold to a large dealer of geraniums in Cleveland, OH.

The large, healthy looking fellow grazing nervously at the back of the herd is the stud bucket, as you might have guessed. His job during the summer months is to protect his herd from the marauding bands of galvanized cans and the dreaded, ugly, flying black plastic bag. As the trained eye can see, the stud bucket is a fine example of a perfectly formed herd sire. He is called "Bubba" and was named "Best of Show" at the annual International Plastic Pickle Bucket Roundup and Sale sponsored by the city of Saskatoon, Canada, last year. "Bubba" will probably be sold at auction at the next international roundup and sale, scheduled for October of next year in Pukwana, SD.

The brood mare of this herd can be seen in the center of the picture, close to the newborn baby dish. She has grown a mane which looks much like the common sofa pillow. The pillow makes her highly desirable out on the ice during the winter months. The breeding of mares with this unusual mane was recently perfected by the Comfor-Seat Ranch in Spink County. The process of breeding is an interesting story and was recently reported in great detail in the *Plastic Fishing Bucket Journal*, June 2002, pages sixty-five to seventy.

Briefly, the *Journal* story tells of early studies in breeding a softer, more user-friendly plastic pickle bucket, which was done in the 1940s. The researchers initiated the early tests in response to requests from skinny-rumped senior citizens who enjoyed ice

Buckets called to duty are one of the most important tools of the avid ice fisherman, who prizes his buckets as a rancher prizes his cattle herd. *Chuck Cecil Photo*

fishing, but found that the strain on their backsides caused unwelcome flare-ups of various conditions, the details of which we shall not discuss at this time.

The flare-ups were made even more uncomfortable by the cold drafts which wafted up off the old, unimproved, bare-bottomed, traditional plastic pickle bucket. The university studies were conducted with grants from the Gedney Pickle Company and general federal pork barrel grants secured because of the political influence of outdoor sport radio voice turned political guru Tony Dean.

A word needs to be said about the economic opportunities for those of you who may be interested in the plastic pickle bucket industry. The demand for plastic pickle buckets by ice fishermen has never been greater. Future pickle bucket ranchers need only a small amount of start-up cash and access to a small backyard of buffalo or blue grass. A small space in a corner of a garage or shed is all that is needed for shelter, since the plastic pickle bucket has, through the ages, adapted to the cold weather, and in fact, thrives on it.

We would advise anyone interested in raising plastic pickle buckets to contact their local game warden, or write to the local Chamber of Commerce which can direct you to established, reputable breeders in the area.

June Postcards

June 1, 1916: Entrance fees to Wind Cave National Park were raised to 25 cents today.

June 1, 1880: Snow fell in Dell Rapids.

June 1, 1949: The first annual meeting of cowboys of the Last Roundup met today in Sturgis.

June 2, 1911: Strong earth tremors were felt in Jerauld County and nearby Gann Valley today.

June 2, 1924: An act of Congress today granted all Native Americans their citizenship.

June 3, 1823: Jedediah S. Smith recited the first recorded Christian prayer in what is now South Dakota.

June 5, 1877: Spectators at a trial crowded into the second floor balcony of a courtroom in Deadwood today, and their weight caused the floor to give way.

June 5, 1877: Fifty attorneys stood in line today to be admitted to practice law before Judge Bennett's court in Deadwood.

June 5, 1924: A Mobridge man called long distance to Philadelphia today and the operators were able to make the connections in just one-half hour.

June 6, 1896: Near Smithwick, eight inches of snow fell today in just eight hours.

June 7, 1941: The USS South Dakota, which became known in WW II as

Sen. Francis Case, left, and Gov. Joe Foss with a model of the USS South Dakota, which in WWII was Battleship X.

Battleship X, was christened today in Camden, NJ, by Gov. and Mrs. Harlan Bushfield.

June 7, 1888: J. W. Coquillette of Miller captured the world championship in the national Hook and Ladder competition today in Pierre. He reached the top of a twenty-six-foot ladder in just 5.5 seconds. He also won the fifty and one hundred-yard runs.

June 8, 1874: General Custer got his marching orders today to explore the Black Hills. After preparations, he and ten companies of cavalry and two of infantry left the fort on July 2 for the historic exploration. He found gold, which caused a gold rush into the Paha Sapa.

June 9, 1972: Extended rainfall and the breaching of the dam on Canyon Lake in Rapid City resulted in a terrible flood that took the lives of 242 people.

June 10, 1955: Alcy Gerard of Chamberlain as of this day had picked a total of 44,000 four-leaf clovers from every state and fourteen counties. Among people to whom he gave the lucky clovers were Herbert Hoover and Dwight Eisenhower.

June 11, 1873: Ten train car loads of buffalo hides and other hides were shipped to Chicago today by rail from Yankton.

June 11, 1884: What is thought to have been the first organized horse race was held in Sioux Falls today at the old fairgrounds on S. Minnesota Ave.

June 13, 1905: George C. Roy of Armour registered the first motor car ever in Douglas County today. The five horse-powered Jeffry with horn and lights was assigned license number 152 and was legal until he had to purchase another license in 1912.

June 14, 1924: Winds reaching speeds of eighty-two mph blew over box cars on the siding at Canning east of Pierre today at about 6 p.m. Unusually high winds hit other parts of the state, killing eight.

June 15, 1927: Pres. Calvin Coolidge arrived at the eastern South Dakota border at sunrise today enroute to the summer White House in the Black Hills. His train stopped briefly in Elkton where he made a short speech before the train continued west.

June 15, 1932: Promotional efforts started today with a Chamber of Commerce-like "Sunshine Squadron" touring the state to promote economic growth, talking up the growing of livestock and community and state development.

June 15, 1889: The Messiah movement and its ghost dance arrived from southern tribes to the Sioux at Pine Ridge and marked the beginning of the final efforts of the Sioux to reclaim their land and their way of life.

June 16, 1938: John Charrlin of Vermillion suffered a heart attack today while working in a field near his home. He made his way to a wood pile and wrote his last will and testament on a shingle. "Give Vera home place-Burnell Farm, John." It was ruled a legal document and is the only will in South Dakota ever filed on a wooden shingle.

June 17, 1944: Eight people were killed when a late afternoon tornado formed in southern Springdale township in Roberts County and headed northeasterly, just missing Wilmot.

June 19, 1879: What were believed to be the last three buffalo in Grant County were shot and killed today near Twin Brooks.

South Dakota buffalo

June 19, 1894: A rainmaker named Jewell, with a $200 advance and $400 more to come if one-half inch of rain fell in Minnehaha County, let loose his chemicals into the air as he had promised county commissioners who hired him. No rain fell, but he warned residents of an impending deluge. The remainder of the month was among the driest ever in the county.

June 20, 1876: Three horse thieves were hanged from a tree on what is still known as Hangman's Hill overlooking Rapid City.

June 22, 1977: Singer Elvis Presley performed his final South Dakota concert in Sioux Falls and died six weeks later.

June 22, 1897: Milbank was mesmerized today when Burt Fuller brought out his new grammaphone and presented a concert of music on it in the Methodist-Episcopal Church.

June 23, 1936: A lightening bolt struck the home of Mr. and Mrs. Thompson of rural Alpena today. It traveled down the chimney, demolishing it, then passed into the bedroom, striking the bed in which the couple were sleeping. The bed was set afire, but the Thompsons were not injured.

June 25, 1876: Nate Love, former Tennessee slave, arrived in Custer enroute to Deadwood for the shooting and riding events in a rodeo there on July 4.

June 25, 1908: The Capitol Building cornerstone was laid today. It contained coins from 1907, the building contract, legislative bills from that year, photographic negatives of the old capitol building, a long list of prominent newspapers, plus messages from current and past governors. The building contract called for an expense of $800,000 plus another $200,000 for furnishings and last minute changes.

June 26, 1856: Ft. Randall was established and work began on structures there.

June 26, 1879: Cornelius Donahue, aka Lame Johnny, a college man and former Homestake Gold Mine bookkeeper, was hanged today on the Sidney Stage Coach line near French Creek. At the time, he was being transported on the stage coach "Old Ironside." A mob stopped the stage, cut Johnny loose from a restraining chain, and hanged him in a nearby tree.

June 26, 1902: A tornado and hail storm stampeded thousands of cattle that had been rounded up during the state's last roundup being held in northern Lyman County.

June 27, 1872: Buffalo Bill Cody and his cream-colored horse visited Ft. Randall. At the time, he was a scout for Capt. Curtis and the detachment of Third Cavalry in the vicinity searching for hostile Indians.

June 28, 1946: The contract was signed for the building of Angustora Dam in Horse Camp Draw in the southern Black Hills.

June 29, 1888: The famous Indian leader Struck By The Ree died today in Greenwood near Vermillion. He was born in 1804.

June 29, 1857: At Lake Thomson, then called Big Dry Wood Lake, a group of Indians from the Yellow Medicine Agency, MN, caught up with Sioux renegade Inkpaduta near DeSmet and killed three of his party.

June 30, 1897: Capt. Hiram Chittenden of the Missouri River Commission wrote in his fiscal report that there was a loss of 395 steamboats since navigation on the Missouri River began and twenty of those wrecks were within the boundaries of South Dakota.

POST CARD
GILBERT

Dear Folks,
   Got here yesterday. All fine.
Weather good. Went shopping
this a.m. at department store.
Saw big rock near here. Very
nice. Home Tuesday. Love,

Lucy

Mr. and Mrs. Art Olson
RFD 3, Box 41

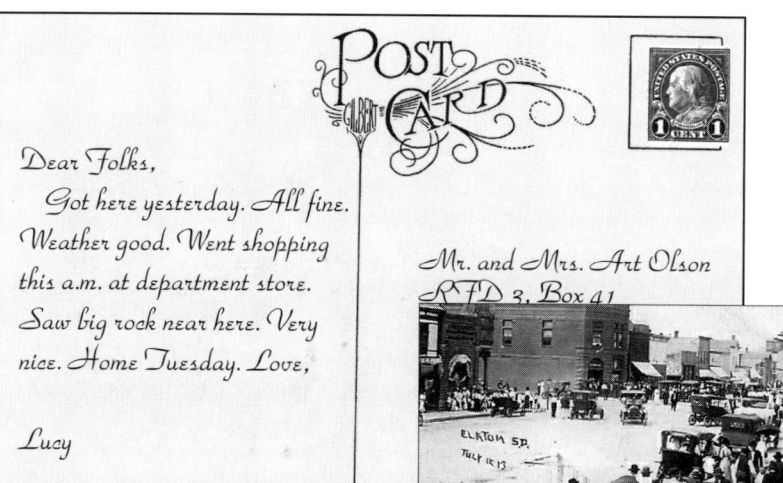

Chapter 14

Glacial Erratics

Chunks of Manitoba, Canada, stand out in Moody and Brookings Counties and help shape the rural skyline.

They were among the tons of rock on gigantic glacial sleds that plowed into eastern South Dakota about twelve thousand years ago. As the glacial ice melted in what is now eastern South Dakota and western Minnesota, the thick, plodding sheet of compressed snow gently, and over many years, lowered its heavy cargo of soil and rocks onto fields in this area. Once in a while, a particularly large rock not ground to smithereens nestled into place. Several can be seen in Brookings and Moody Counties.

Some of that glacial baggage has been picked from fertile fields by generations of South Dakotans intent on protecting plows and cultivators as frost brings up a new crop of rocks each year. These small rocks,

Dr. Donald Berg of South Dakota State University and the massive glacial erratic known since pioneer times as Lone Rock. It is located in a pasture in eastern Moody County and believed to be the largest glacial erratic in South Dakota. *Donald Berg Photo*

and some even the size of bushel baskets, have been thrown with disgust into the irregular rock piles that now dot the landscape.

More of what was picked up and carried down from the Hudson Bay area into what is today called the Coteau de Prairie has been put to good use as building material, from rock garden borders to elaborate walls, homes, and barns. Strong-shouldered pioneers walking beside the skidding stone-boats, and modern-day farmers on front-end loaders, removed the never-ending emergence of glacial rocks that popped to the surface under the pressure of freezing and melting sub-soil.

A portion of Manitoba's rocky terra firma has become practically invisible, ground to tiny, microscopic bits by the glaciers' movements, so that it is the consistency of flour. Today it provides some of the minerals valuable in the production of crops. But once in a while, the rocks win out over the unbelievable forces of glaciers and man.

Several known examples of glacial rocks that survived the crushing pressure of glaciers and have defied man's removal efforts can be found in Brookings and Moody Counties. All five of these huge rocks are called "erratics." They are composed of what is known as pink granite. At least three are known to exist south of Aurora, and two other giants can be found east of Flandreau about a mile south of Highway 34.

The heavyweight of the five is known as Lone Rock. It sits in ponderous repose in a cow pasture east of the picturesque Lone Rock Church in eastern Moody County. The big Lone Rock east of Flandreau is the largest "glacial erratic" known to exist in South Dakota, according to Dr. Donald Berg, associate professor of geography at South Dakota State University.

This old photograph of the so-called Trenton Rocks south of Aurora shows the size of the two glacial erratics in the early days. The horse's head is about where the land surface around the rocks is today. Debris and fill have been added to the rocks' base through the decades, and this, combined with soil eroded by winds that settled in among the debris, slowly built up the surface. The land on which the rocks are located was homesteaded by the James Pike family. In the early days, travelers from the Canby, MN, area used the rocks as a landmark. *Aurora Centennial Book Photo*

Lone Rock is easily viewed from a county road. It looms above the surrounding prairie about a mile off Highway 34 in the eastern part of the county. It can be seen east off the graveled road. Lone Rock in Moody County is about twenty-five feet high and forty paces around. Berg estimates that it might easily weigh in excess of one hundred tons, with possibly another fifty or seventy tons of it below the ground. But that's just a guess. Like an iceberg in a sea of grass, no one knows how deeply into the soil this particular boulder is embedded.

Another Moody County erratic is about a half-mile west of the huge "Lone Rock," near the Lone Rock Church. It may have broken off from its big brother during the centuries-long, tumbling trip down from Canada.

North of the Moody County boulders, two glacial erratics in Brookings County are located near Aurora. Another, smaller boulder is two miles southeast of those two. No one can say for certain, but they all might be a part of a package of huge boulders broken off by the glacier as it crept down from Canada. The two side-by-side glacial erratics of the Brookings County trio lie south of Aurora in Trenton Township. They are about one and one-half miles south of the paved road to Elkton, or more specifically, in the northwest quarter of Section 26, Trenton Township. The two rocks, one several times larger than the other, are known as the Trenton Rocks.

The third Brookings County rock, considerably smaller than either of the Trenton Township Rocks, can be seen in a slough along the east-west gravel road about two miles from the Trenton Rocks.

Orville Gab of the South Dakota State University Geography Department stands between the large and the smaller glacial erratics located south of Aurora in Brookings County known as the Trenton Rocks. The larger rock shows the ravages of numerous lightening strikes through the years. Considerable debris has been thrown around the rocks for decades. Note the size of the rock in the photo on the previous page taken in pioneer times. *Donald Berg Photo*

Berg thinks that all of these rocks were carried down from what is now Manitoba, Canada, by a finger of a glacier several hundred feet thick. The glacier, known as the Wisconsin Drift, helped form what is now the Coteau de Prairie, which is an amoeba-shaped, hundred square mile of high plain composed of miscellaneous rocks and soil debris that spread out underneath the glacier. Today the Coteau averages about 1,700 feet above sea level and extends southeastward across northeast South Dakota and some of southwest Lincoln County in Minnesota. Berg said that the Coteau and the big rocks in Brookings and Moody Counties were probably born during the Pleistocene Epoch.

The Trenton Rocks south of Aurora easily stood out above the prairie during the early years of settlement. But through the years, debris has been thrown around the bases of the two rocks. Dust in the 1930s and since then has filled in between the rocks and debris. Over the decades the ground level around the Trenton Rocks' bases has been raised perhaps five or six feet. Charlie Wilber, who grew up in the area and now lives in Miller, said he remembers the Trenton Rocks because they were very near the Wilber farmstead. He recalls that rocks and debris from a razed building foundation on the farm were dumped at the base of the Trenton

This large glacial erratic is in a slough about two miles southeast of the Trenton Rocks in Brookings County. It is much smaller and is not as well known as its cousins, the Trenton Rocks. *Chuck Cecil Photo*

Rocks. No doubt small glacial stones, birthing from the frosty sub-soil in the surrounding fields, were also carried to the site and dumped around the Trenton Rocks. Photographs in this chapter show how much the soil has been built up around the rocks.

Dr. Berg said that in the pre-settlement days, the rocks were used by Native Americans as guideposts and sighting towers to scan the landscape for buffalo, other game, or possibly approaching enemies. Pioneers also used the rocks for guideposts, and later, the larger rocks became popular sites for picnics and neighborhood celebrations. Climbing the rocks was a popular pastime for pioneer children and adults alike, offering a magnificent view of the immediate area.

Buffalo found the rocks convenient rubbing rocks, as cattle in the Lone Rock pasture do today. The larger rocks show the ravages of nature, with large cracks at their tops, probably caused by lightening strikes at some point in the past.

The Wisconsin Ice Age can be visualized as the glacial cake frosting that was slathered on the final layer of rock, gravel, and sand mixtures on the Coteau, over the droppings and debris left by earlier glacial sheets. So Lone Rock and its smaller compatriot and the Trenton Rocks and their little cousin about two miles away are visual reminders of the awesome power of the thick-iced glaciers of eons ago. The snow of perhaps a thousand or more winters accumulated and packed the lower levels of snow so tightly that glacier ice formed. More winters dropped more snow, and the weight started the snow pack on its long, gravity-powered, bulldozing glide south.

As the glaciers moved along, they scooped up Canadian land and rock, ground some to fine powder, and carried the powder and rocks, large and small, to eastern South Dakota and parts of southwestern Minnesota on today's Coteau de Prairie. An example of a glacial rock field, probably the same one which deposited the glacial erratics this chapter discusses, can be seen about a mile west of the I-29-Madison turnoff on Highway 34, on the hilly, north side of the road. This boulder field continues south and can be seen along I-29 for about two miles beyond the highway's intersection with Highway 34.

Some believe that history will repeat itself and that other glaciers will form over the ages. They will probably follow the earlier glacial paths, perhaps bringing other erratics down to South Dakota. Possibly, the awesome power of the next glacier might even move the Trenton Rocks in Brookings County and Lone Rock in Moody County to entirely new locations.

UNITED STATES POSTAGE
1 CENT

Dear Joyce, We went hiking yesterday to a place called Rim Rock. Very pretty. Too tired to write. That back pack was too heavy for a petite girl like me. See you soon
Shirley

Miss Joyce Hansen
RR 3, Box 18

RIM ROCK TRAIL

Chapter 15

Backpacks and Book Straps

Have you noticed what kids are carrying to and from school these days?

We're talking elephantine, Antarctic expedition-sized backpacks. We understand they're needed so kids can keep up with assigned homework.

I wonder if schools still have such a thing as a "study hall." It was set aside as a period for study. That's when I remember doing work on the following school day's assignments. The only backpack I ever owned was an old, beat-up hand-me-down with the smell of moth balls that I used for aid and comfort on Boy Scout fourteen-mile overnight hikes up in the hills to meet a merit badge requirement.

But unfortunately today, the ubiquitous backpacks are as much a school status thing and keeping up with the Joneses as they are carriers of important school stuff. Pity the poor child whose parents can't afford a fancy pack.

Status and fads are big-time happenings among teens these days, and now the universal demand by kids for backpacks has made merchandisers giddy because they are "the thing" up and down the busy halls of grade schools. Even children three and four anticipating school and mimicking their older brothers and sisters want a backpack. Teachers have made L. L. Bean stockholders very, very happy.

Backpacks are now as much a part of K-12 culture as wearing baseball caps backwards, pulling baggy

A backpack with a young child attached boards a school bus for the long ride home.
Chuck Cecil Photo

pants down as far toward China as is humanly possible according to all laws of gut and gravity, then walking on the frayed cuffs, starting and ending sentences with "like," and early morning caffeine binges from the myriad of gaudy soda pop machines in public school hallways, the proceeds from which line the deep pockets of Douglas Draft and Steven Reinemund, wealthy CEOs of Coca Cola and Pepsi.

Even kindergarteners are into the backpack act, for gosh sakes.

Their little kindergarten backs are bending under their little kindergarten packs laden with heaven knows what a kindergartener needs at school.

We're told the backpacks (in prehistoric days they were called knapsacks) are K-12 necessary because of homework assigned. I have nothing against homework, except that it has brought on this unintentional skeletal consequence called the backpack stoop. Now we not only have youngsters who are overweight or obese, but they also walk with a stoop.

Homework, I suppose, is good, and if none were assigned, I'm sure parents would object to that, too. But there needs to be equilibrium here. Homework today far exceeds homework of yesterday when study hall helped ease the burden. How in the name of Nobel Prizes, I wonder, did students since time turned a corner at the pyramid ever make it through school without a backpack?

Sure, they had homework. But it didn't come out of the maw of a fancy, expensive, stylish backpack. Then, a backpack was something you tied on the backs of mules, carrying supplies and ammunition for the advancing cavalry.

At best, students for most centuries past used a length of frayed rope to hold books together on the long walk home. A fad did develop when old belts replaced frayed ropes. We called them book straps. No child today would have the foggiest idea of what a book strap is.

Many students in days past didn't even have book straps because they didn't have belts, either. They had to learn how to carry books the old-fashioned way, known as the "hand carry."

Yet, despite being backpack deficient, they managed to learn their lessons and later contribute greatly to the good of society.

In a recent television report on the backpack fad, we were told that health officials are concerned about what the packs are doing to the growing bones of our nation's children.

The film clip showed kids of all ages, shapes, and sizes, struggling along bent nearly double like an Indonesian peasant carrying a massive load of hay to the barn, except our kids were toting the bloated carcasses of a backpack to class.

They carry, I'll wager, much more than the necessary accoutrements of education. There are probably tubes of lip gloss, combs, tissues, car keys for their cars, car keys for their parents' cars, gel pens with neon ink, ID cards (some their own), dollars for the pop machine, Pokemon cards, a cellular telephone, designer water, a discman with headphones, and possibly a change of clothes.

You and I know that if you give kids an empty container, they will hunt around like squirrels in the fall until they find a sufficient supply of "stuff" to fill it to the brim.

In the television clip, I saw that some of the kids had progressed beyond the humble backpack. They were pulling along those up-scale wheeled suitcases you see tooling around airports. You can surmise from this that the kid has too much stuff, and also, that the poor kid has parents with plenty of extra money but very poor judgment.

If we carry this progression of backpacks on to the next generation, it is only a matter of time before small golf carts stuffed with homework assignments are weaving in and around the pop and candy machines in school hallways.

Can the small pickup truck be far behind?

Let's hope that the old book strap makes a comeback and will be considered, like, cool once again.

POST CARD

Place the Stamp here
ONE CENT
...ates
...ssions
...and
...TS
...gn

Greetings from
Brookings
Went bullhead fishing and
caught a bunch in S. Riv.
Will eat tonight. Come see
us sometime.

Hattie and Jim

Hiram Walker, Jr.
North of Volga

Chapter 16

Bullhead Demise

Bullheads, from my long experience as a mud-bottomed, yellow-bellied nimrod, are an awful lot like house cats. They really don't care much about anything but their own comfort, and they have minds of their own. Bullheads swim in the slow lane and they do it in very slow circles so they don't get lost. They are at the bottom of the fisherman's preference list, except in Nebraska, where they are considered a top game fish.

Until recently, we've had what I consider a good balance of wit-matching bullhead fishermen and the bullheads themselves here on the flatlands. But then the mega-sports/hunting store opened its gate in Mitchell, and Cabela's fans from thousands of miles away now think nothing of a jaunt to Mitchell's Mecca to spend their money on gimmicks they believe will improve their successful pursuit of wildlife, including bullheads.

Cabela's, when it opened its massive doors, said that about 1.5 million customers would visit the store along I-90 on the south side of Mitchell each year. I think that number has been exceeded by far. Satellite businesses have grown up in the Cabela's neighborhood, too.

The two-acre store has over 250,000 different items on its shelves, which sure doesn't bode well for the mentally handicapped bullhead. In the past, even if the yellow-bellied fish was a sandwich shy of a shoreline lunch, it could compete with the lug-nut sinker fisherman like me. When I was a kid, my tackle box was an empty pocket or, on important forays into the bush, an empty one-pound Maxwell House coffee can.

Bullhead fishing novices didn't use fishing poles. We just cranked up our throw lines like David with his slingshot and let fly for the giants that squirmed in the mud and muck on the bottom of prairie stock dams. If you were lucky, your throw-line, weighted down with a pound or two of rusty nuts and bolts, sailed out over the water in slow motion circles.

Accidents did happen, however, and from time to time the missile headed in the opposite direction, toward our old gray '36 Chrysler that my dad drove until after WW II, or toward the spot exactly between the eyes of my beady-eyed little brother standing well back from the cast.

On a successful cast, a fist-full of hook-loaded grasshoppers tied to that twirling, whirling throw-line plunked into the water. It would set a herd of bullheads to licking their lips like dogs at a Methodist picnic.

We used an old, smelly gunnysack as a creel to hold our catch while we tried to catch some more. Sometimes, we'd get forty or fifty pounds of bullheads, all to be cleaned the old fashioned way, by nailing the critters through the head onto a board, incising the blue skin with a sharp knife to get a pliers-jaw grip on it, and then skinning them head to tail before clearing out the innards.

The more ostentatious bullhead fishermen back then used a telescoping casting rod made of steel. He probably had in his pocket the rusted pliers he'd use later for cleaning, and he had a dirty jackknife. To bullhead purists, the use of specialized equipment like that in the quest for fish seemed a tad unsportsman-like, especially when the prey has about half the brain one would find in a barrel of hair.

I don't imagine you can find a throw line, a gunny sack creel, or a set of nut and bolt sinkers at the new Cabela's store in Mitchell. Today's fishermen need the latest in equipment to catch what we did in the old days with cast away, everyday items.

Young, SUV-powered, jog-with-a-dog, sweatband and fanny pack fishermen of today day say it isn't the catch, but the challenge of the catch, that they pursue. Sure. Sure. If that were the case, Cabela's would be selling yellow, bricklayer snap string for throw-lines and ten-foot bamboo fishing poles.

If truth be known, today's nimrods are in it for the numbers just as we were.

Why else, in the name of Tony Dean, would they put their faith in gimmicks like radar detectors, sonar echo equipment, boats as big as Aretha Franklin or the USS South Dakota, robotic minnows that have bowel movements on demand, trained fish that herd others from isolated spots on the lake to where your line is cast, and three horse-powered motorized reels that plug into your car's cigarette lighter?

Numbers! That's why.

To be frank, I've been somewhat concerned about the future of bullhead fishing in South Dakota for years. Now, my hopes for the survival of this slab-sided, ugly species have been shattered with the opening of that Cabela's store the size of Cameroon right at our back door. I mean, they sell everything there but birth control pills for field mice, for gosh sakes.

It won't be long before out-of-town fishermen from Nebraska get dressed up in their fancy blue fishing bib overalls and load up with expensive fishing devices at Cabela's before heading out to the bullhead holes we know and love so well. Time was when Nebraskans didn't spend a dime in South Dakota on fishing, bringing their own lunches and sleeping over in the back seat of their cars to save motel money. We called them "Blue Whistlers" because of their tight fistedness, their dress, and the way they whistled in disbelief when they learned that a dozen minnows in South Dakota bait shops was going to cost them a dollar.

Caught up in the mystique of Cabela advertising gimmicks, those Nebraska Blue Whistlers will just flat clean us out of every bullhead in the state. Then, where in the name of Izaak Walton will our local kids with their nuts and bolts throw lines go to catch the wily bullhead?

 July Postcards

July 1, 1942: The Army Air Base at Sioux Falls welcomed its first troops for training today. Before the camp closed on Jan. 1, 1946, an average of twenty-thousand men a year would be stationed there.

July 1, 1877: As of today, Deadwood officially had seventy-five saloons.

July 1, 1913: Ninety-one veterans of the Civil War from South Dakota were on the battlefield at Gettysburg, Pa., for a month-long fiftieth anniversary observance. Transportation in a special train was provided free to the veterans by the Chicago, Milwaukee and St. Paul Railroad. Capt. Newton Kingman of Selby organized the trip.

July 2, 1939: Mt. Rushmore was officially dedicated with the unveiling of the head of Teddy Roosevelt. Western movie star Tom S. Hart entertained the crowd of twelve thousand. The monument cost $989,992.12, of which only about $25,000 came from donations from residents of the Black Hills.

July 2, 1895: Howard's flour mill exploded today and burned to the ground. Three people were killed.

July 3, 1905: After three days of rain, another cloud burst in the upper Bad River valley caused flash flooding in Ft. Pierre. Eight died and eighteen more were washed downstream but rescued.

July 3, 1906: Today is the birthday of the cow College Belle Wayne at South Dakota State University. College Belle became a record milk producer at five years of age and continued to produce prodigious amounts of milk until her death in the fall of 1924.

July 3, 1919: The entire town of Whitewood turned out at Oak Park and filled the grandstand to honor returning WW I veterans. The day ended in tragedy when a severe storm struck and lightning killed two and injured several others who had gathered to welcome the men.

July 4, 1886: A rail line reached Rapid City, and on July 14, the first train arrived from Pierre after a fourteen-hour trip.

July 4, 1877: The first dance ever in Lead took place in the Paul Jentzer Store, and the entire female population of Lead attended. Miners kept all eight women on the floor for the entire evening.

July 4, 1930: The carved likeness of the head of President George Washington was unveiled by President Herbert Hoover today at Mt. Rushmore. For the first time, the phrase, "Shrine of Democracy" was used by one of the speakers.

The head of George Washington is nearly completed on Mt. Rushmore. The partial head of Thomas Jefferson has been blasted from the left side of Washington and is beginning to appear in its new location in stronger granite on the right side. *C&NW Railroad Co. Photo*

July 4, 1914: Art Borne, trying out his new airplane at the Deuel County Fairgrounds near Clear Lake, was able to fly only a fourth of a mile at fifty feet, and due to malfunctions, nearly hit a telephone pole. On landing, Borne crated up the plane and shipped it back to the Minneapolis manufacturer.

July 4, 1903: After first being barred from Aberdeen because city fathers worried the trucks carrying heavy elephants would ruin the wooden block paving, the entry parade was re-routed and the circus enjoyed its best day of receipts ever.

July 4, 1913: Snow fell at Cedar Butte in Mellette County today.

July 4, 1876: Nate Love, who was a famous black cowboy in the Black Hills, took first place today in the first Deadwood rodeo that became part of the Days of '76 celebration still held. He won the roping contest in a time of nine minutes and took home $200 in prize money. Six black cowboys competed in the roping event. Love later became a train porter.

July 4, 1916: Ivy Baldwin, a tight rope walker, crossed 1,800 feet above the huge Open Cut at the Homestake Gold Mine in Lead today. It was a walk of 450 feet. He ended the day by parachuting from a hot air balloon.

July 4, 1908: Oscar Nelson of Huron today won the world's lightweight boxing title, knocking out Joe Gans in the seventh round in a bout in California.

July 4, 1886: Over one thousand Indians came to Miller today to help the town celebrate Independence Day.

July 4, 1912: The first motion picture in Jones County was shown today at Monson School near Van Metre. It was *Custer's Last Stand*.

July 4, 1946: A 17-year-old Pierpont boy, Selmer Mortenson, rode his horse 160 miles in six days, arriving today in Mobridge in time to see his first rodeo.

July 4, 1902: Corn froze on the stalks in fields in the Marion area today.

July 4, 1933: Judges and promoters of the Timber Lake Bathing Beauty Contest were disappointed when no entrants signed up for the much-advertised contest.

July 4, 1887: Gen. Hugh Campbell of Yankton was guest speaker at Armour's first Independence Day observance. He spoke for two hours. He wasn't invited back.

July 5, 1936: The hottest temperature to date in South Dakota was recorded today in Gann Valley: 120 degrees.

July 5, 1914: A tornado-like cloud in Deuel County dropped red shingles on area fields. No one in the county had red shingles, so residents assumed the cloud had carried them at least fifty miles in the air from another county.

July 7, 1908: Dan Mosier today killed the famed White Wolf in Hay Canyon near Smithwick after chasing it for seven miles. Veteran hunters in the area had been trying to kill the she-wolf since 1895.

July 7, 1910: The only two automobiles in Lake Norden, owned by Alfred Kinnonen and Martin Winjam, collided at the Iver Roisum corner in town today.

July 8, 1922: Henry Shriever reported that when a tornado struck his home in St. Charles today, a lighted lamp was lifted from the table and deposited on the floor, still lit and undamaged.

July 9, 1938: A tornado northeast of White struck at 6 p.m. and picked up six horses belonging to Dick Miller. Francis Farrell saw them circling in the sky above him. They were carried over two fence lines and were set down with such force that all were killed. One dead horse was literally planted in a field, still in a standing position buried up to its knees.

July 10, 1907: The first town lots in Wall went on sale today. As part of the event, a man named Winteringer of Hartington, NE, was to make a hot air balloon flight. He and a barber from Yankton imbibed before the flight, and while drinking, managed to talk the local banker, who was also celebrating in the bar, into making the trip with them. The flight went off without a hitch, and when the balloon was found later near Sage Creek, all three men were found unhurt and sober.

July 10, 1939: The famous McVay Burn in the Black Hills started in the intense, 102-degree heat of the day. It burned for four days and destroyed 21,859 acres of timber. Over 1,200 men battled the fire.

July 13, 1882: Thomas Egan became the second man hanged in Dakota Territory today when he was executed for the murder of his wife. It took three tries through the trap door before he died. He was the first man executed in Minnehaha County.

July 14, 1920: An earthquake described as mild hit the southern Black Hills, breaking windows in Custer and Hot Springs.

July 14, 1873: Thirty-one Norwegian families arrived to settle the area around Lake Hendricks in Brookings County, SD, and Lincoln County, MN.

July 14, 1904: Ninty-seven residents of Bruce went on a train excursion today to Watertown to see the Ringling Brothers Circus.

July 14, 1931: The famous South Dakota bucking horse Tipperary made his last public appearance today at the Belle Fourche Roundup Rodeo. The horse first performed in 1918.

July 16, 1915: The famed W. S. Peck Band of Watertown won top honors at the National Elks Convention in Los Angeles, CA, today.

July 17, 1925: The American Legion Baseball program was born today in Milbank.

July 17, 1952: Today, the first sighting in South Dakota of an Unidentified Flying Object (UFO) was reported in Rapid City.

July 17, 1913: The Clear Lake city council voted today to install a water trough for horses on main street, and another nearer the ground for thirsty town dogs.

July 17, 1936: A young boy, Billy Timms of Hawthorne, NJ, was bitten by a rattlesnake today while touring Wind Cave National Park with his family. He recovered, but his mother suffered a mild heart attack during the ordeal.

July 18, 1870: A twenty-minute storm hit Ft. Wadsworth (Sisseton) today. One trooper was injured, 1,200 panes of glass were broken, and a company barracks was badly damaged.

July 20, 1904: The Battle of Bonesteel took place today. During registration for the drawing for Rosebud Reservation land, a fight broke out between law-abiding citizens and gamblers who had invaded the city. The citizens drove the gamblers out of town after they tried to disrupt the registration process.

July 21, 1885: The first annual meeting of the South Dakota Press Association was held today in Watertown. The newspaper owners would continue to call their group the "press" association until the late 1900s when television and radio announcers begin referring to themselves as "the press," too, causing some confusion. The association is now the South Dakota Newspaper Association.

July 21, 1884: Miner County's worst hail storm to date struck in mid-afternoon. Jagged chunks of ice pierced roofs and broke windows. A farmer south of Carthage reported that his team of horses each had one eye knocked from their skulls by hailstones.

July 21, 1951: Movie and television star Cheryl Ladd was born today in Huron.

July 21, 1884: A rural school house in Highland Township, Minnehaha County, which was occupied by the teacher and twenty-one students, was blown one-half mile during a violent wind storm today. The sliding building remained intact on its journey and no students were injured. Later, members of the school district voted to leave the school house at the new site.

Cheryl Ladd

July 22, 1930: Using lanterns to light the way, Ted Buffington took the first tourists on a guided tour of Wonderland Cave north of Rapid City.

July 23, 1911: James (Scotty) Philips, the popular Buffalo King, died on his ranch near Pierre today. His estate included ten thousand acres of land, six thousand cattle, and seven hundred head of buffalo.

July 23, 1925: The famous wolf Two-Toes died of injuries after a sixteen-year career of killing what ranchers estimated to be $50,000 worth of livestock in Butte County. Clyde Briggs shot and wounded Two-Toes and was transporting him to town when the animal died. The wolf lived a charmed life. It once led the Haivalo boys on a chase covering 140 miles, and another time, a relay of seven horsemen failed to run Two-Toes down.

July 23, 1878: Jacob J. Goossen died today while attempting to rescue his wife, his parents, and a child, all of whom were stranded on the roof of their sod house one and one-half miles north and one-half mile west of Marion, during flooding on the Vermillion River.

July 24, 1944: Triplets Theresa, Mary Anne, and Marcella were born today to Mr. and Mrs. Omer Nelson of Groton.

July 24, 1884: John Erbe of Edmunds County, who lived near Ipswich, shot four rifle balls into a few buffalo on his land, and killed one. It was believed to have been the last buffalo killed east of the river. Erbe sold the meat for 12 and one-half cents a pound to Ipswich residents.

July 25, 1927: Gov. William Bulow attended the first annual Deuel County Old Settlers Picnic today and presented a special certificate to the county's first permanent settler, B. J. Cochrane, after whom Lake Cochrane is named.

July 25, 1951: Somehow, two and one-half-year-old Darrell Halse of Clear Lake climbed up the city water tower and had to be rescued by John Heiney of Gary today.

July 26, 1877: Grasshoppers hit Sanborn County today, swarming in from the east with the roar of a hailstorm. They ate everything but the grass for twelve miles along the James River, then abruptly left three days later. Trees stripped bare by the hoppers started to green up again in September.

July 26, 1922: Thieves entered the Holabird Bank at 2 a.m. today and exited nine times. Eight explosive devices were set off before the ninth charge finally opened the safe. Concerned townspeople who heard the explosions watched cautiously from their homes. The burglars made off with about $1,000 in cash. They paused outside of town to cut telephone lines, but were later caught near Kimball.

July 27, 1881: A man named Dal Cooper was accidentally shot and killed today by a Ft. Pierre dance hall girl, the local newspaper reported. It appears that the crowd was all "pretty full" and were shooting off their revolvers through the roof and sides of the house when Cooper got in the way.

July 27, 1917: Asher Knepper and his family arrived in Redfield where he began work on his new tractor design. It became the most unusual tractor ever: a round ball with an engine inside that caused the ball to roll. It did not sell well.

July 28, 1925: A live tarantula was discovered in a bunch of bananas at the Lane General Store in Lane. The large spider was placed in a glass jar and displayed in the store for several weeks until it died.

July 28, 1916: As automobiles became more common, the Strandburg town board ordered all hitching posts on main street removed, with the exception of one left standing in front of the hardware store.

July 28, 1904: South Dakota's last frontier opened to homesteaders today with drawings for land in Gregory County. Over five thousand registered, then waited in tents and small shacks at Burke for their names to be called. At the same time, twelve saloons opened for the first time in Bruke.

July 31, 1892: The idea of a Corn Palace in Mitchell was discussed today after a prototype in nearby Plankinton attracted the attention of Mitchell residents. The first palace was built in 1892. The present Corn Palace was built in 1920.

POST CARD

Place the Stamp here
ONE CENT
United States
and Possessions
a Canada and
Mexico
NO CENTS
or Foreign
1 CENT 1

Hi dear friends:

We drove as far as Yellowstone today. Two flat tires. Went over this road. They call these pig tails, and did I ever squeal when George nearly went off road. I like straight roads like back home in Brookings C. Geneva

Mr. and Mrs. Ronald Hand
RR 3, Box No. 14

Chapter 17

Pickled Hogs' Feet

How about those robbers who walked off with 52,000 pounds of raw, unpickled hogs' feet? Did you read about it in the paper?

The feet were scheduled for shipment to Hong Kong, but someone stole the whole truckload.

What in the name of a hamper full of hocks would inspire someone to abscond with over twenty-five tons of hogs' feet? Maybe we're all missing something here.

Truth is, until I read in the newspaper about this feat, I'd never really given much thought to the feet of hogs, except to ponder why pigs, heavy with lard and hams and sausage, seemed to walk around on their little, dainty tippy-toes.

I've seen smeared-up jars of pickled pigs' feet on the back shelf in bars but never considered them to be something I'd enjoy eating. Ugly cloven cadavers float around in a mawkish brine from which a bubble might break loose and scurry up to the foam-thick surface from time to time, scudding up from the algae-covered bottom.

I'm not exactly a bar fly so I haven't seen it all, but during all of my years of viewing pickled pigs' feet at bars, I've never actually been present when one of them was ordered and eaten. I assume that takes place late at night when customers' judgments become somewhat flawed.

It never dawned on me that there were actually people on this planet who ate paws of pig. A drunk maybe, trying to impress a girl or win a bet. But I figured the jars of percolating porcine were there in the bar mostly as conversation pieces, like the Budweiser painting of Custer's Last Stand and the pickled eggs bobbing for room in another dusty, crummy-looking jar on the back of the bar.

I asked a friend who knows hogs how many pigs 52,000 pounds of hog feet represented. As soon as I asked, I knew it was a dumb question, since that would depend upon how big the pigs were at the time they were "defeated," so to speak.

The value of this particular stolen load of hog feet bound for Hong Kong was said to be $35,000, or about sixty-seven cents a pound. Knowing of the public's desire to learn more about hog feet at every opportunity, I visited the grocery store to do hog foot research and check on the current price of pigs' feet. The store didn't carry raw hog feet. It did have pickled feet, stuffed tightly like dill pickles in little nine-ounce jars on the shelf. The price for the jar full was $3.75 a pound.

Maybe the raw, untreated feet are only in vogue in this country on a particular holiday, like the anniversary of the invention of the stomach pump.

The store did stock hocks, which, as I understand the anatomy of a hog, is a part located just up the block from the feet. The meat experts I checked with figured that a fair market value for a raw foot of hog might run you $1.29.

I've always assumed that a pig's cloven hoof was a solid object. I figured they were the material used for buttons or dice or artificial teeth. But as far as I can tell upon close examination, the hoof is like a toenail. The protocol of hog foot eating is that before you eat the pickled foot, you simply peel off this toenail and throw it away.

I checked around for more information on pigs' feet and was surprised that in addition to pickling the hoof, you can also bake it, broil it, fry it, roast it, fricassee it, and even jelly it. Interestingly, in every recipe I checked, the first line was "wash the foot thoroughly." Helloooo?

American restaurants have successfully marketed the lowly chicken wing by slathering it with sauce and renaming it a Buffalo Wing, after the city of Buffalo, NY, where the idea originated.

Restaurants serve fish by calling it "sole" on the menu.

So why not a new restaurant food using pigs' feet?

It could be sold as sole of feet.

Dear James and Dorothy:
The Black Hills today. Deadwood
tonight and then back to Rapid
City to catch the train. Bus tour
today into Needles. This is eye of
same. Thank you again for feeding our livestock. We'll do it for
you next summer. Your neighbor
The Smiths

PS We saw some mountain goats
today and Jim says he may trade
his cows for them.

Mr
RR

Chapter 18

Pygmy Goats Coming to Brookings

It was nearing April Fool's Day, and I wrote this exclusive, unfactual, unsubstantiated report for the local newspaper. Surprisingly, many people didn't catch on until they came to the very last sentence. The story went like this:

It's on good authority that a West River rancher wants to establish a pygmy goat ranch north of Brookings.

Ordell M. McDonald, 67, of Dupree, is looking for suitable East River land. He needs about three square miles that would become an open range for up to thirty thousand pygmy goats which he would raise.

The goats, which stand about fifty inches when fully grown and weigh in at about twenty pounds, are in great demand on the West Coast where they are considered ideal pets.

Californians also like the goats because of their fine wool, sweet milk, and tiny hooves. Of course, Californians also like bean sprouts and seaweed, so go figure.

McDonald explained that raising an exotic animal such as the pygmy goat is something he's always wanted to do. He said the idea came to him one hot day when he was mucking around in one of his cattle feedlots, fighting off flies while knee deep in smelly cow caca.

He said he chose the Brookings location for his ranch because of the goat expertise available at South Dakota State University and at the Brookings Elks club, where a herd of crabby old goats stop in each evening for refreshments and to bleat a bit.

He also said the Swiftel Center in Brookings impressed him. "The little critters are so small we could stage the entire National Pygmy Goat Show out there in that foyer," he said, picking his teeth with a swizzle stick.

After looking at several available farms in the area, he returned to Dupree to care for his cattle, but expects to return to Brookings next week to meet with the Brookings County Commission about any potential problems he might encounter with zoning laws. "As far as I can tell, there isn't anything in the zoning laws that would prohibit pygmy goats, but I could be wrong."

"You've got to remember that anything negative about pygmy goats is so small and inconsequential that it would be hard to write a law about it," he said. "For example, you could put a day's worth of manure from a thousand pygmy goats in one of those fancy flower pots you've got bolted to your main street light poles."

So he doesn't expect any problems with zoning. "Pygmy goats are known for cleanliness," he said. McDonald explained that if a pygmy goat's diet is supplemented with activated charcoal, its manure has very little odor to it. "Shucks, you hardly know they're around, and it doesn't stick to your boots, either. How about them apples?"

One problem that local officials said needed to be worked out was the immense size of the herd. Even with their tiny amount of scat, the goats' tiny hooves could tamp the droppings into large, hard-pan areas through which rain or snowmelt could not penetrate.

McDonald said that he's thought about that, too, and one way he figures he can solve that problem is to erect fences and form smaller pastures so the herd is dispersed. He didn't anticipate the fencing to be prohibitive so far as cost was concerned. "Heck, for pygmy goats, it only has to be about two feet high."

Milk from the pygmy goats is a highly sought item in California communes. Cheese made from the milk, which will be processed in the Volga or Lake Norden cheese plants, has many uses other than food. It is used by the National Aeronautic and Space Administration as grease for lunar and planetary exploration vehicles.

"It holds up really well," he explained. "It don't bind like your regular cow cheese." NASA likes the cheese-grease because in a pinch, astronauts can eat it. "But that would be only in an extreme emergency," McDonald advised. "It can cause the trots in weightlessness," he said, "and for a space guy all zipped and bolted into a space suit tight as an Irishman at a Catholic wake, that wouldn't be much fun now, would it?"

Once McDonald has a herd established in Brookings County, he expects to hire a large crew of milkers, perferrably women. "They have smaller hands and more patience with tiny creatures," he said.

Wool from the goat herd is used to make sweaters for children, and the meat is highly recommended for people on diets, since the servings are so small.

Hooves are used by the gaming business. They are made into dice. The hooves also are used to make little combs and barettes in doll sets, and they are also in demand for manufacturers who make buttons for concertinas and accordions.

The only known enemy of the pygmy goat is the striped gopher. But McDonald doesn't think this will be a problem. He said he's found a guy in Montana who raises and trains pygmy llamas with an aversion to striped gophers.

"I'll probably buy a couple dozen to sprinkle in with my herd," he said as he accidentally poked himself in the eye with his swizzle stick.

The first trainload of pygmy goats is expected to arrive here next April Fool's Day.

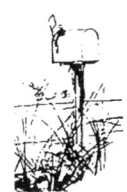

August Postcards

Aug. 1, 1855: The steamship *Kate Swinney* was wrecked between Vermillion and Elk Point. It was the first sinking of a steamship in what is now South Dakota. The 328-ton sidewinder was loaded with furs bound for St. Louis.

Aug. 1, 1876: Pony Express services to the Black Hills began today from Ft. Laramie and Sydney to Deadwood. The trip took a team of riders forty-eight hours.

Aug. 2, 1876: Jack McCall shot Wild Bill Hickok today. He was hanged at 10:10 a.m. on March 1, 1877, near Yankton, for the crime.

Aug. 2, 1922: A total of 4.29 inches of rain fell today in Mellette County in less than four hours. Bridges on White Thunder and Butte Creeks were under water.

Aug. 2, 1933: Gov. Tom Berry called a special session of the Legislature and 3.2 beer was declared legal for sale as a result.

Aug. 3, 1958: Oahe Dam on the Missouri River was closed and began impounding water.

Aug. 4, 1903: Rev. Charles B. Clark officiated today at the funeral of Calamity Jane at the Deadwood Methodist Church. Rev. Clark was the father of Badger, who later became South Dakota's poet laureate.

Aug. 4, 1927: Pres. Calvin Coolidge, in the Black Hills for the summer, today was given the Sioux name "Big Chief Stone-In-The-Face" by Chief Chauncey Yellow Robe.

Construction of Oahe Dam's huge water intake chutes. *SD Highway Publicity Photo*

Aug. 5, 1881: Brule leader Spotted Tail was shot and killed by Crow Dog today.

Aug. 6, 1900: Martin Charger, a Cheyenne Agency Sioux, died today. Charger gained fame for leading a group of young Indians which elders called "Fool Soldiers" to the rescue of several white women and children from hostile Sioux near the mouth of the Grand River in the early 1860s,.

Chief Spotted Tail's abandoned home provided by the government. *Submitted Photo*

Aug. 6, 1903: The elegant, $25,000 Waldorf Hotel in Andover opened tonight. The forty-room showcase was advertised as the best hotel this side of Minneapolis. An orchestra came by train each week to provide dinner music for Sunday guests.

Aug. 7, 1875: Charles LaGrange, who was the first Sisseton Indian agent, was killed in his home today when lightening struck as he placed a pan beneath a leak in his roof to catch the rain water seeping in.

Aug. 7, 1874: General George Custer killed a grizzly bear today at Nahant on Rapid Creek above the present town of Rochford as he led an exploratory contingent of cavalry through the Black Hills.

Aug. 7, 1926: Lubber, said to be the world's largest horse, was among the many attractions at the second day of the two-day Homestake Golden Jubilee in Lead. The horse was twenty-one hands high and weighed three thousand pounds.

Aug. 8, 1901: Ernest Lawrence, who would win a Nobel Prize in physics, was born today in Canton. He invented the cyclotron, which, in turn, made possible the making of the atomic bomb. The 103rd element, Lawrencium, is named in his honor.

Aug. 8, 1877: The *Deadwood Champion* newspaper condemned the behavior of Calamity Jane today, calling her a "fraud and dead give away" and concluded that "a hundred water girls or mop squeezers in this gulch are her superior in everything."

Aug. 8, 1882: Mrs. Matt Gorder of rural Frederick, enroute to town for help with the impending birth of her third child, was unable to reach the community and gave birth alone on the prairie to the first child born in the community. The boy was named Frederick.

Aug. 10, 1955: Either Mr. C. L. Bell, his wife, or daughter Pamela of McDonald, KA, was the one millionth visitor to Wind Cave National Park.

Aug. 10, 1941: Sam Moses, former sheriff of Fall River County who later became a range detective, died today. In 1891, the South Dakota Stock Growers hired him to catch rustlers, and he nearly broke the association's bank because of the rewards he received for his successes. As a sheriff he once chased a murderer, Henry Smith, for four months, traveling about three thousand miles into Old Mexico to capture Smith and return him to Cheyenne for trial.

Aug. 10, 1875: The town of Custer was laid out today, and its main street was made wide enough to allow eight yoke of oxen and the wagon to make a U-turn.

Aug. 11, 1879: Shacknasty Jim died of gunshot wounds today after attempting to escape from jail at Ft. McKinney, Wyoming Territory. He and Bill Cole had been jailed there after capture on the Powder River by U. S. Scout Fred Hans, who had trailed the horse thieves after they took seven cavalry horses from Ft. Meade in Sturgis, Dakota Territory, on July 20.

Aug. 12, 1929: Alfred Kray, who ranched near Rosebud, was bitten by a rattlesnake today. He saved his life by lacerating the bitten area with his knife.

Aug. 12, 1909: Amanda Clement of Hudson today broke the world's record for long distance baseball throwing by a female. She was umpiring a game in Parkston and afterwards threw the ball 227 feet, which was thirty-four feet longer than the previous record.

Aug. 13, 1929: Mrs. James Jewett of rural Lemmon reached down today to pick up a pantry rug and a rattlesnake struck at her arm. It missed. She grabbed a broom and swept the snake right out her front door.

Aug. 14, 1873: Christian Frech was born in Alsace-Lorraine today. He came to South Dakota to settle on a farm near Lebanon in Potter County, and invented a washing machine that he manufactured and sold for $4 each. It is said that Frech drove his 1928 Model A Ford for fifty years.

Aug. 15, 1937: Six people, including four youths ages twelve and thirteen, drowned today in Lake Amsden near Andover today.

Aug. 17, 1962: President John Kennedy dedicated Oahe Dam today. As the Washington press plane departed the Pierre airport after the ceremony, the jet's blast blew away a huge section of asphalt patch work on the runway, but the aircraft was able to take off.

Aug. 17, 1880: *The Signal* newspaper of Ft. Pierre reported today that two men ran a race in downtown Ft. Pierre last night. The cause? A few revolver shots.

Aug. 17, 1954: The world premiere of Walt Disney's *The Vanishing Prairie* was held in Hot Springs today.

Aug. 17, 1901: At the first militia encampment at Huron today, Sgt. Hunt and Pvt. Mackey of Clark each suffered the loss of a hand by the premature discharge of a cannon.

The cannon that misfired and injured two Clark National Guardsmen is now located in the cemetery in north Watertown. *Chuck Cecil Photo*

Aug. 18, 1874: The first threshing machine in what is now South Dakota worked the Andrew Hogstad farm in Minnehaha County. E. J. Berdall was straw boss for the crew of the machine owned by Martin and Eric Trygstad of Lake Campbell in Brookings County. The crew would work its way north that fall, ending the harvest season in Brookings County.

Aug. 19, 1945: Myron Floren of Day County today married Brdyne Koerner of Sioux Falls.

Aug. 20, 1876: Preacher Smith, who prayed at Wild Bill Hickok's funeral, was found shot to death today on the road to Crook City. Minutes before his death he had completed a street sermon in Deadwood and then tacked a note on his door which read: "Gone to Crook City and if God is willing, be back at 2 p.m."

Aug. 20, 1954: President Dwight Eisenhower today signed Public Law 776 that granted the Cheyenne River Sioux payment of $10.6 million plus relocation costs for lands lost to the Oahe Dam.

Aug. 21, 1958: Peter (Frenchie Pete) LaFlamme, who hauled Wild Bill Hickok's body to the Deadwood Boot Hill cemetery for burial on Aug. 3, 1876, died today at Alva, WY. Frenchie Pete was hired to exhume Wild Bill's body and others and move them to the new Mt. Moriah Cemetery.

Aug. 21, 1900: Jon C. Waldron of Ft. Pierre was born today. He would later be killed leading his famous Torpedo Squadron Eight in the early stages of the Battle of Midway during WW II. While the squadron lost all fifteen planes, the squadron's efforts are said to have influenced the successful outcome of the battle.

Aug. 21, 1806: Lewis and Clark today entered what is now South Dakota today on their return trip down the Missouri River.

Aug. 24. 1950: Prairie artist Harvey Dunn gave his collection of prairie art to the people of South Dakota to be held in perpetuity and displayed at South Dakota State University, where Dunn was once a student.

Aug. 24, 1885: Hugh Glass, explorer and trapper, was mauled by a bear today and left for dead on the Grand River. Stripped of his clothing and equipment by others with him who assumed he was deceased, he regained his senses later and somehow managed to crawl and stumble one hundred miles to Pierre to survive the ordeal.

Aug. 24, 1865: Henry Buskala, who would be remembered as the man who brought the first miner's hard hat to Lead, was born today in Finland. The hat was made of laminated strips of wood.

Aug. 25, 1885: *Little House on the Prairie* author Laura Ingalls today married Alonzo Wilder in DeSmet.

Aug. 25, 1922: Four escapees from the state penitentiary shot and left for dead three law enforcement officials, including Jones County Sheriff Jay C. Babcock, States Attorney M. L. Parish, and J. A. Robertson, after the trio stopped the convicts near Stamford, Jones County. The four were later apprehended north of Wall. One was killed in the shoot out there, and the other three were returned to the penitentiary where they served until released in the 1940s. All three injured law officers survived.

Aug. 26, 1876: Ft. Wadsworth today was renamed Ft. Sisseton.

Aug. 27, 1901: Clydia Becker Richardson was born today in Highmore. She would become the first female Keeper of the Seal of the United States of America in 1943 in Washington, D. C.

Aug. 28, 1909: F. R. Ginther purchased the first automobile in Morriston today. It was a one-cylinder and had a chain drive.

Aug. 28, 1936: Franklin D. Roosevelt's nine-car train arrived in Aberdeen today at about 4:30 p.m.

Aug. 28, 1943: David Soul, movie and television actor and the star of *Starsky and Hutch*, was born in Sioux Falls today.

Aug. 29, 1976: President Gerald Ford visited Rapid City today.

Aug. 29, 1881: The state's first artesian well was sunk 460 feet down at Yankton before hitting what was described as a "gusher."

Aug. 30, 1874: General Custer and his troopers returned to Ft. Abraham Lincoln near Bismarck today, ending the Black Hills expedition that took the explorers on a 1,205 mile round trip, entering the Black Hills on July 24, 1874.

Aug. 30, 1920: An earthquake, the second in forty-five days, was noticed in the southern Black Hills today.

Aug. 31, 1879: Otie Arbogast, a Hand County pioneer who had one ear chewed off by a bronc he was breaking, died today.

Aug. 31, 1943: A WW II bomber over the bombing practice range in Jerauld County near Wessington Springs crashed today on the range, killing all crew members.

POST C

Hello Mother and Father:
   Here's a picture of grandma
in her retirement. She said she
may get a stick and play golf,
or chase cats with it. She's
fine, but forgetful sometimes.
Home next week.
   Verdean

Chapter 19

Retired and Golfing

Retirement is when you don't have to get up at any certain time in the morning, and if you do, you have to check your notes to remember why you made such an early rising.

I've asked newly retired friends of mine how they manage to find things to do during the day. Invariably the response is that they are busier than ever.

There are hardly enough hours in the day, they say.

They take a new interest in life's little things, usually pastimes with inconsequential meanings, such as golf.

They become so addicted to golf that every detail of every game is burned into their rapidly-diminishing minds. They may have difficulty remembering their wedding anniversary dates or what year car they are driving or where it is currently parked. But they somehow amass an enormous store of minutely-detailed knowledge on their golf games.

Freed-up brain tendrils once dedicated to profit and loss information, employee insurance plans, and Chamber of Commerce meeting dates now light up like clanging pachinko machines when the subject of golf comes up. As they recall "the game," blood rushes to their ears, the lobes of which are fighting the never-ending and losing battle with gravity. Jowls sag but don't waddle quite as much when they talk about their games.

Retired men are able to remember what happened on the seventh hole fairway the day Enron collapsed. Information on golf bubbles up from their brains' golf globules with military precision and soapy profusion.

For instance, the men were having coffee and talking about the game they played on Saturday, June 19, 2001.

* Temperature, 78 degrees
* Wind, five MPH from the SW, gusts to 15
* Dew point, 53
* Altitude at ball's location, 1,762 to 1,764 feet above sea level
* Surface—Ball in fescue two and one-fourth inches high. Dandelion about three weeks old, budding, located four feet to left of ball, making footing difficult. Shoe size, 9.5, one cleat missing near big toe, left shoe.
* Distance to cup, 133.79 yards

* Club—Five iron, needed cleaning

* Distractions—Sound of airplane overhead. DC-9. Heading NNW at eight miles a minute, probably out of Chicago for Seattle. Four minutes behind schedule. Used earplugs. Partner coughed, but quietly said "excuse me."

Then someone at the table asks the golfing raconteur:

"Who were you playing with?"

The retired golfer pauses and strokes his chin, following the overhead fan in its slow cycle. He hums quietly and fumbles with his drink straw.

"Ah, it was my best friend. Known him all my life. Let's see. Who was it. Well...it was...does it really matter? I can prove my score by showing you the scorecard filed away down in my locker. Wait a minute. I'll get it."

Five minutes later he's back at the table.

"Can any of you guys remember my locker combination?" he asks.

But they don't even hear him because in his brief absence another epistle came up, and they are now discussing a new golf remembrance. The one played on June 19, 2001, is, once again, history.

The game on July 31, 1999, has taken the country club's center stage, and the current act is the sand trap on the ninth hole which was a duck slough when the course was built back in 1933.

Or was it a stock dam?

Maybe it was built in 1953.

Where did Joe park his car?

TUCK'S POST CARD

CARTE POSTALE.

POSTKARTE.

By Appointment.

Helen and Joe: They had a parade here today and then a dance after, but I did not go because I had to work. Heck. Band was good, but not as good as ours at home. Miss you all. Be home soon. Love JC

(FOR ADDRESS ONLY.)

*Hermanson Family
Rural White, SD*

Chapter 20

Rose Hair Oil

I can still smell the aroma of Rose Hair Oil in its squat little bottle with the black plastic cap. We bought it at the Five & Dime Store for a quarter or so.

I probably got a half-pint of the stuff for that twenty-five cents, but it was used liberally in my high school days, so it sure didn't last long. It tended to build up behind your ears, so some mornings, you could recycle a few spoonsfull from there.

Slathered on, it made my black hair glisten like a plastic-covered silage pile on a sunny afternoon. My hair was so aerodynamically coifed it could withstand a force five hurricane.

One winter, tooling along on my clamp-ons at Wilson Park Ice Rink, I spotted fellow sophomores, the Trout twins, Jean and Joanne, gliding along hand-in-hand up ahead near the pond's brick outlet. They were pretty good lookers and they lived near Rapid City's then upper-crusty West Boulevard. I decided to make my move in the interest of my future work-free well-being and eventual plush, and early, retirement. With twins, I figured my chances were at least fifty-fifty.

In preparation for this chance encounter I pulled out my nine-inch, barber-approved comb and drew it through my beautiful Rose Hair Oil-immersed hair. Engrossed as I was in making myself more handsome and debonair than Clark Gable, I didn't see little Freddie Schick speeding along off to my portside.

Freddie really was a little guy. Unfortunately, someone had dropped him when he was a baby, and the fall injured his back. He was about two feet tall, but a genial, popular kid who became famous as a Cobbler cheerleader smaller than the megaphone he bandied about at basketball and football games. He went on in later life to run the state's police radio headquarters in Pierre, and was a popular, effective leader of that important arm of the law.

Freddie eluded our collision without a scratch and went skimming on past, while I plowed unceremoniously into the rink's brick outlet with my arms waving in reverse. I hit the bricks and scratched my hand and broke my wristwatch. The most damage was to my pride, however. For the remainder of my high school years I was reluctant to make my Trout twin move for fear they had witnessed that very embarrassing Wilson Park Ice Rink pileup.

Life went on. The summer after I graduated, the Korean War started. I joined the Navy to avoid the draft. Preparing for my adventure, I sold my 30-30 deer rifle for $60. I planned to buy a new wristwatch with the money. But I made the mistake of waving it around down in The Hole, a pool hall hangout under the Buell Building in downtown Rapid. There were probably fifty kids down there at the time, and if you emptied the pockets of every one of them, you wouldn't have $60. I was flat-out rich for my age and for the times. But that didn't last long.

My long-ago collision mate Freddie Schick saw the two twenties and two tens and challenged me to a final, farewell game of snooker with a $50 bet. Freddie used a wooden Orange Crush pop case to stand on when playing snooker, and sometimes had to actually crawl onto the playing surface. He was good, but anyone worth his weight in cue chalk should be able to beat a guy who needed to stand on a pop case to hit the cue ball. Looking ahead, I planned to buy an even better watch than the victim of my Wilson Park crack-up with my newfound fifty dollars.

But Freddie beat me rather handily. It was not even a contest. My two twenties and a ten spot fluttered reluctantly into his pop case. So much for a wristwatch. I headed for the Five & Dime to buy Rose Hair Oil with my last $10 because, bound for exotic ports of call and beautiful ladies dancing in grass skirts on every Navy pier the world over, I couldn't be sure Rose Hair Oil would always be available. So I bought a big supply and took them wrapped in towels with me to San Diego and nine weeks of boot camp.

But before I knew what was happening, the Navy barber shaved my head, and the Chief Petty Officer in charge of Company #748 told me to dump the Rose Hair Oil. Instead, I packed it in my ditty bag and headed for nearby Tijuana, Mexico. At that time, it was not illegal to smuggle anything into Mexico, especially Rose Hair Oil.

I figured I could either sell it or trade it for a taco or a ticket to the bull fights. I found a cab driver and explained in halting Spanish what I had. He answered in perfect English that he had a nearly new watch he would trade me. He said it was "diamond-encrusted." I still needed a nice watch, thanks to the ice rink collision with Freddie Schick years ago. So long, Rose Hair Oil.

The next day I noticed that my diamond-encrusted watch had stopped running. A shipmate who knew something about jewelry discovered that someone had used oil in the mechanism to make it run better. If wound tightly, it would kick in for about five minutes, then seize up. He also told me the diamonds were fakes.

A few weeks later, the Navy arranged buses for a free trip to a football game in the Rose Bowl at Pasadena. I wore my useless, diamond-encrusted watch and my thirteen-button dress bell bottoms to impress the Trout twins or whomever would be the University of Southern California cheerleaders at the game.

Outside the stadium, a guy was selling colorful Rose Bowl souvenir programs for $5, which I didn't have. But I had my nice Mexican watch. I hitched up my bell bottoms, wound up my watch, set the time, and as it ticked its short life away, sidled up and offered to trade the watch for a program.

"It's diamond-encrusted," I pointed out, glancing over my shoulder just in case the Military Police had me under observance for transporting contraband over the Mexican border.

The trade was made, and I lost myself in the crowd.

But I don't recall what happened to that souvenir Rose Bowl program. And I now have misgivings about using all that Rose Hair Oil as a kid.

Unfortunately, I think I used too much of it all through high school. My head got so slippery that most of my hair has just flat slid off and headed south, for Tijuana, I suppose.

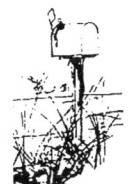 September Postcards

Sept. 1, 1925: The Rosebud Bridge over the Missouri River near Wheeler was opened today.

Sept. 1, 1900: Col. Theodore Roosevelt, governor of New York, visited Aberdeen.

Sept. 1, 1925: Three men robbed the Whitewood Bank at gunpoint, leaving with about $2,500.

Sept. 2, 1911: Free rural mail delivery (RFD) began today in the Smithwick-Oral area near Hot Springs.

Sept. 2, 1927: Charles Lindbergh flew over Deadwood this morning, then buzzed Lead and Spearfish.

Sept. 2, 1918: The National All-American Field Trials for bird dogs were held today in Mobridge.

Sept. 3, 1917: The Sioux Falls Stockyards opened today. It would become one of the nation's largest.

Sept. 4, 1886: Triplets were born today to Mr. and Mrs. Jacob Sellers in Bear Butte valley, the first born in the Black Hills. The girls were named Maude, Elsie, and Sarah. The family had previously consisted of two sets of twins.

Sept. 5, 1898: Verne D. Mudge was born today in Campbell County. He would later become a major general and command the 1st Cavalry Division in its successful march to Manila, The Philippines, in WW II after landing at Lingayan Gulf. He was wounded by a Japanese hand grenade during that campaign.

Sept. 5, 1929: Lt. John A. Winefordner of the 1st Pursuit Group, 94th Squadron, was killed today when his aircraft crashed during the dedication of the Lemmon Municipal Airport.

Sept. 5, 1947: A huge prairie fire in Hyde County burned five hundred square miles of central South Dakota farm and ranch land today.

Sept. 6, 1913: Charlies Kerlin, young Mellette County bachelor who worked at the 909 Ranch, won first place today in the first annual Mellette County Fair canning contest held at Wood.

Sept. 7, 1899: The Buffalo Bill Wild West Show was in Watertown today.

Sept. 8, 1892: The Sinai Temperance Society was organized today, and Article III levied a fine of $1 against any member breaking the abstinance pledge.

Sept. 11, 1886: Rapid City Street Railway Company's first car rattled down the tracks on Main Street for the first time today. The line operated for nineteen years.

Sept. 11, 1951: A roundup of wild horses in the Wind Cave National Park resulted in the capture of twenty-six.

Sept. 13, 1844: Capt. James Allen of the 1st Regiment of the U. S. Dragoons, accompanied by four officers and fifty-two men, made a military reconnaissance into Dakota Territory today from Ft. Des Moines. They reached the site of present day Sioux Falls and reportedly were very impressed with the cataract on the river, then at flood stage.

Sept. 14, 1963: Four girls and one boy were born to Mr. and Mrs. Andrew Fischer in Aberdeen today.

Sept. 15, 1959: Glen Austin Powers, a twenty-seven-year veteran of the U.S. Post Office and the northwest route out of Burke from 1921 to 1948, died today. He once used a postage stamp to patch a flat tire experienced on his rural route mail car. It held until he was able to reach a nearby farm where a more permanent patch was glued on.

Sept. 17 1937: The granite head of Abraham Lincoln was unveiled at Mt. Rushmore in ceremonies today.

Sept. 19, 1902: Ernest Loveswar was hanged in Sturgis today for the murder of George Ostrander and George Puck, who were killed while in camp near Red Owl. The first time the trap was sprung, five of the nine rings in the hangman's noose slipped, so six minutes later he was hanged again.

Sept. 19, 1906: Ben Reifel, who would become the first Sioux Indian elected to the House of Representatives in 1960, was born today in Parmalee on the Rosebud Reservation.

New South Dakota Rep. Ben Reifel is sworn in by House Speaker Sam Rayburn.

Sept. 18, 1925: The last roundup on the famed 160,000-acre Mulehead Ranch near Bonesteel ended today.

Sept. 21, 1876: The City of Deadwood was organized and taxes set, including a tax of $5 per doctor, $10 per druggist, and $15 for gambling licenses. Operating a dance hall required payment of $20.

Sept. 23, 1863: Henry Bohnhoff of Gettysburg was born today. He later became a butcher, and it was said that he was so used to riding his horse-drawn meat wagon that in his later years when he switched to a truck, he always rode in it with one leg hanging out the door to facilitate a quick exit in case it got away from him.

Sept. 25, 1876: The Gilmer and Salesbury Stage Line made its first run between Cheyenne, WY, and the Black Hills. The trip took forty-eight hours and the price for a ticket was $30.

Sept. 26, 1878: The stage from Cheyenne to Deadwood was held up by highwaymen today near what would become the South Dakota-Wyoming border. Two passengers were killed, and thieves made off with $25,000 in gold dust.

Sept. 27, 1966: The long-awaited Platte-Winner Bridge linking the Rosebud and East River was opened today. The bridge is over one mile long.

Sept. 28, 1908: Democrat William Jennings Bryan was in Mitchell today. Republican William Taft visited town the next day, followed by Prohibitionist candidate Eugene Chafin.

Sept. 28, 1942: Rapid City Air Force Base, later Ellsworth, was activated today. It first was a training ground for B-17 crews and in 1987 became a base for the B-1 bomber.

Sept. 29, 1885: Author Hamlin Garland, who would later win a Pulitzer Prize, walked into the Treasurer's office in Leola today and paid taxes of $17.13 on his claim in the SW quarter of Section 32, Twp. 125, Range 67 near Ordway, valued at $575. He would later write *Main Traveled Roads* and over twenty other popular books.

Sept. 30, 1920: An earthquake today rattled dishes in cupboards for twenty minutes in the Tripp area.

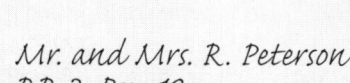

Hi All. They sure grow grain out here and men are scooping it all day. They even gave me a shovel, but I didn't get much done because Harmie talks all the time. Enjoying my summer and will be home in fall. See you.

Dean

Oh, by the way, make sure my little brother doesn't get into my stamp collection.

Mr. and Mrs. R. Peterson
R.R. 3, Box. 12

Chapter 21

Official State Scoop Shovel

During the legislative session in 2001, a bill was introduced to change the state's nickname from "The Mount Rushmore State" to the more inclusive "Monument State." I thought we were the Coyote State.

Changing our nickname in 2001 was a dumb idea then and in my humble opinion, remains so today.

Some legislators have the habit of arriving in Pierre with an insatiable appetite to enact a law to make something the official state something or other.

I don't know. Maybe it's the water in Pierre. Or maybe it's the thought of just being stranded out there far from any hint of civilization for a couple of snowbound months.

Whatever it is, our state is filling a very large official book with official somethings or other. It's all a waste of time.

For example, the 2003 legislative session approved a bill to name rodeo as the official state sport, another ridiculous waste of legislative time and taxpayer dollars. After all, how many bull riders live on your street?

A few years before that, kuchen became the official state dessert, if you can swallow that. The only people in South Dakota who have ever eaten kuchen, or have any idea what in the world it is, live in Eureka, which, if we'd put an exclamation mark behind it, could be the official state response from anyone winning the lottery.

And would you believe South Dakota even has an official state dirt? It's Hoedek, for reasons known only to our state's soil scientists. For all of the rest of us dummies, who cares? Dirt is, by gosh, dirt.

We have dozens of "official" designations, even an official fossil, which, surprisingly, isn't the guy at the bar down at the Elks Club having a few shooters. Our official state fossil is the Triceratops, which still leaves room for legislators at some future date to come up with an official state dinosaur, although I hope they don't fiddle with that, which incidentally is our official state musical instrument.

Most South Dakotans never even knew the state was nicknamed "The Mount Rushmore State." Most assumed it was still "The Pheasant State" or "The Sunshine State." We apparently dropped the term "pheasant state" when someone figured out that it might not look good for a state to have an official bird which citizens enjoyed killing and then eating.

The "Sunshine State" moniker was tacked on in 1909. It was then pried quietly off in 1992 when some busybody legislator decided to give the state a new nickname, "The Mount Rushmore State."

One reason was that Florida already claimed "The Sunshine State." Another unmentioned reason, I'll wager, is that to refer to South Dakota as "The Sunshine State" would be like calling Minnesota "The Land of 514 Lakes."

To be perfectly honest, if the nickname is to reflect a state's image, South Dakota should probably be called "The Blizzard State," although chances are North Dakota has already laid claim to it.

So after the Sunshine State and the Rushmore State, along comes a group in 2001 who lobby to rename our state "The Monument State." They argued at hearings in Pierre that there are monuments at Mt. Rushmore, at Crazy Horse (which will be a work in progress for several thousand years), and at the Corn Palace in Mitchell. They overlooked another monument, that being the boondoggle called the Dakotadome in Vermillion, which recently had to have a new metal roof applied to replace the one made of cloth. That new $12 million roof cost more than the entire original building, which incidentally was a bad idea to begin with.

Crazy Horse isn't all about a monument, of course. It's also about a family patriarch's employment plan for his offspring down through the ages. It was an ingenious idea fifty years ago when the blasting started on the mountain that was to become a likeness of Crazy Horse, although there are no photographs of Crazy Horse to pattern it after.

Crazy Horse will continue to be a good idea for the centuries that will be required, using well-timed dynamite explosions, to complete the project. Meanwhile, adjunct tourist attractions crop up on the Crazy Horse grounds like mushrooms in a manure pile, with plans for a university campus among a plethora of other tourist attractions out there near Custer.

The Corn Palace isn't really a monument to my way of thinking, but a building onto which ears of corn are stapled. While not a monument, it is a giant bird feeding station and a mecca for polka dancers.

I do have an alternative to "The Mount Rushmore State" or "The Monument State" ideas. What's wrong with South Dakota being known as "The Scoop Shovel State"?

A scoop shovel is a beautiful and functional object. Show me a South Dakota garage without a scoop shovel dangling from a rusty nail and I'll introduce you to someone who's just moved to South Dakota from Alabama.

The shovel's smooth, flowing lines, fine metal patina, and wooden handle worn smooth as a baby's behind make it a masterpiece in my mind.

It would look good mounted over the fireplace, reproduced on license plates, crocheted on feed sack towels and davenport pillows or, in a smaller version, made into classy lapel pins made of Black Hills gold imported from China and sold at Wall Drug.

The scoop shovel conveys an image of the agricultural bounty to which we are all beholden. It would not be difficult to find at least one scoop shovel on every square mile of South Dakota's Hoedek soil. We have more scoop shovels in South Dakota than we do Norwegians, school districts, or lawyers.

When pioneers first came to this state, slogging through gumbo up to their knees and fighting off mosquitoes, they brought with them the handy scoop shovel. It was useful for moving the grain they would grow, for clearing the dust of the Dirty Thirties that seeped into the kitchen, and it was a great snowbank destroyer.

With a hard knock between the ears, scoop shovels could convince a stubborn horse or cow to do about anything the shoveler desired. It was extremely efficient in picking up spattered barn messes, and it sent thousands of rattlers to that great den in the sky.

Farm kids used them for sleds in the winter, either tied behind a horse or car, or riding one on the hint of a hill down by the creek.

Farmers who retired and moved to town usually sold all their farm tools except one. They kept their faithful scoop shovels. It is South Dakota personified.

So my advice is to take up an old scoop shovel and heave those tourist industry-inspired state nickname suggestions right out the screen door.

BLOOM BROS CO
SCENIC
AMERICA

POST C

Mom and Dad

*Having a grand time. This is
Ad. Byrd's ship he used to
plow through the ice. I got sea
sick on it and got off in a big
hurry. Hope you survived the
blizzard last week. Fair is like
nothing I've ever seen. Love
James*

ADMIRAL BYRD'S
SOUTH POLE SHIP
CHICAGO
WORLD'S FAIR
1933

Chapter 22

Beautiful Snow for the Birds

Hundreds of eastern South Dakota residents head south when the north winds blow and scurrying snow scratches at the door. We call them "snow birds" and, out of ear shot behind some sand dune on the Arizona wasteland, they call those of us who like South Dakota winters a tich on the fuzzy-headed side of life.

You can recognize snowbirds from the small sofa pillow and bright orange afghan tucked neatly up on the back window shelf of their automobile as they motor south.

An elderly couple we know spent a few winters in Mesa, AZ, then grew tired of the fast pace there and decided to remain in South Dakota for the winter. The gentleman kept a revealing diary.

Dec. 8, 6 p.m.—It started to snow, the first snowfall of the season. The wife and I took our coffee and sat by the window, watching the soft, fluffy flakes floating down around us. You sure won't see such a sight in Mesa. It was beautiful. God's inspiring winter show. Our little poodle, Buster, sat entranced on the wife's lap, barking joyfully at the swirling flakes outside. What an enjoyable day.

Dec. 9—We awoke to a big, beautiful blanket of crystal white snow covering our landscape. Wow! A fantastic sight. It must inspire poets. Every tree and shrub was coated with a beautiful white robe. I shoveled snow for the first time in many years and I loved every minute of it. I did the driveway and made a little path back to the alley and our garbage cans, which looked like Dairy Queen cones with the snow piled high on their tops. I even scraped away a little spot for Buster to use when we let him out at night before we all three retire after the reruns of *Gunsmoke*. James Arness as Marshal Matt Dillon is our favorite actor and Buster barks whenever Festus limps onto the screen. That Buster is something special to us.

Later today, we were so happy to see the city snowplow came by. The blade moved snow on our sidewalk and driveway. It was slightly compacted in large, heavy chunks, but were pleased that it was out of the street. So I happily went out and shoveled again. Buster, wearing the little red sweater my wife made for him, enjoyed a second romp in the snow. I showed him where he should go that evening when we let him out.

Retiree Virgil Stenberg, who lives on an acreage six miles west of Flandreau in Moody County, kept his sense of humor during a recent harsh winter. His rural home is barely visible in the background behind a giant snow bank. *Chuck Cecil Photo*

Dec. 12—The sun has melted our lovely snow. Oh, well, I'm sure we'll get more before this beautiful Dakota winter is over.

Dec. 14—It snowed eight inches last night and the temperature dropped to a minus twenty degrees. Shoveled the driveway again, but decided the path to the alley wasn't really necessary. Took out the garbage, but couldn't get the lids off the cans. The damn snow cones had melted and the water refroze over the lid's edges. Decided that Buster needed to be more independent, so didn't shovel a spot for him, either. The city snowplow just came by, and now the sidewalk is covered with what appear to be blocks of ice, some weighing fifty pounds or more.

Dec. 15—Went to the car dealership and traded in our van for a used 4x4 truck. Bought snow tires for the wife's car.

Dec. 17—Still very cold outside. Took vehicles in to get new anti-freeze checked. Damaged the oil pan on wife's car driving it over the ice blocks the plow had purposely deposited on our driveway.

Dec. 20—We had another fourteen inches of that &*(@#!% white stuff again today. Had to force the front door open against a monster snow bank, but with my wife's help, we succeeded. Wife in bed now. Says her back is wrenched from the pushing. I went out and did more shoveling. Decided the sidewalk didn't need clearing from edge to edge, but did make a little path for the paperboy and the mailman. The darned snowplow guy came by again—twice. I called the service station and they came out and got our cars started. Found Buster after several worrisome hours. We'd let him out last night and he became disoriented, I suppose. Found him frozen solid to the metal on one of my

Virgil Stenberg didn't see much of his pickup truck until the spring thaw. *Chuck Cecil Photo*

snow shovels I'd accidentally thrown on "his spot." We cleared the snow away from him and chopped him loose. The poor thing is still whimpering, in bed with the wife, who still can't stand up straight. What a sight for sore eyes Buster was. I'd never have found him except I was digging around in the snow trying to find the newspaper the careless carrier boy threw at our door from the path on the sidewalk. Who raises those kids, anyway?

Dec. 22—We will have a white Christmas because the guy on TV said thirteen more inches of snow fell last night. I wonder why he smiles when he says that, the jerk. Got all bundled up in coveralls and overshoes to go out and shovel, but decided I needed to go to the bathroom and had to strip down again. Wife is still in bed. So is Buster. He's also reluctant to let me know he has to go to the bathroom.

Dec. 23—If I ever catch that blankety-blank-blank who drives the snowplow I'll bury his weasel-hide in a snow bank. I think he sits in his idling snow plow down the street and just waits for me to finish clearing our driveway. Then he comes barreling up at sixty miles an hour and dumps a load on it. I threw my shovel at him today after he gave me a smarty-pants one-fingered salute and a big grin as he drove by. I missed, but one of the plow's tires ruined the shovel so now I am down to the little plastic one that came in the snow kit I bought at the hardware store.

Dec. 24—Merry Christmas Eve. The forecast is for twenty inches of that white junk and high winds tonight. That mealy-mouthed, fat TV weatherman talks about it like he's happy it's coming. Does he have any idea how many shovels full twenty inches of snow is? If he'd shovel like I have he wouldn't be so fat. That wiseacre snowplow guy came by asking for a donation to the city hockey program. I returned his salute of yesterday and wished him a happy holiday. As I did I could hear Buster growling from beneath the covers in the wife's bedroom. Some protection he is, the worthless, ugly mongrel.

Dec. 26—We were snowed in on Christmas Day and I finished off the last of the "Christmas Cheer" yesterday. Felt a little lonely. Wife is still bedridden and Buster is staying close to her, so I watched some *Gunsmoke* reruns, took down the Christmas tree, drank a little and wrote a nasty letter to the mayor.

We got more snow, if you can believe it. Car was towed away because I left it parked in the street while I ran into the house to get my gloves and go to the bathroom. Cripes, I was only in the house five minutes or so. What's the big deal? Called the mayor and complained. He just laughed, the SOB. I wouldn't be surprised if he's related to that snow plow jerk.

Dec. 27—Called the real estate office to list our home, but the walks were filled with snow so they couldn't come see it to tell us how to proceed. Maybe tomorrow. Picked up some brochures from the travel agency today.

Jan. 1—The New Year came in with more snow. I just cleared enough from the driveway so I could ram the car through the snow banks. Got stuck twice, but finally made it out. Headed south on the interstate at eighty MPH for Arizona, but when I was about twenty miles from home I realized I'd forgotten something. So turned around and went back to get the wife and her wimp of a dog, what's his name.

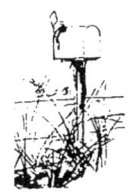 October Postcards

Oct. 1, 1896: Henry Heintz, former legislator and Elkton farmer who became Elkton postmaster, today filed for a patent on his airship and received patent #607,561.

Oct. 1, 1889: Pierre was selected as the temporary site of the state capitol in the constitutional election, winning over Huron, Watertown, Sioux Falls, Mitchell, and Chamberlain. In 1890 it was chosen permanent site over Huron.

Oct. 1, 1889: The South Dakota Constitution was adopted by a vote of the people.

Oct. 1, 1872: The locomotive "Judge Brookings" crossed over the Big Sioux River today on the Dakota Southern Line from Sioux City, the first ever in Dakota Territory.

Oct. 1, 1934: Lawrence Welk and his Fruit Gum Orchestra played this evening at the Webster Pavilion.

Oct. 1, 1929: Airmail service between Milbank and Watertown began today with one plane flying the route each day.

Oct. 1, 1889: Arthur Mellette, the last Dakota Territorial governor, became the first governor of South Dakota today.

Oct. 2, 1939: Dennis Brady, the man who in 1909 wrote a law banning the sale of cigarettes in the state, died today in Kimball.

Oct. 3, 1906: The first Aberdeen motion picture theater, the Bijou, opened today.

Oct. 3, 1928: John Philip Sousa's band today presented a concert at South Dakota State University in Brookings.

Oct. 3, 1908: Two youths hunting rabbits near Sioux Falls accidentally fired into a powder house, setting off three thousand pounds of dynamite and one hundred kegs of black powder. The bodies of the boys were never found.

Oct. 3, 1863: Dakota got its nickname of Coyote State after a horse race at Ft. Randall between entries from Iowa and South Dakota. Iowans said the winning South Dakota horse "ran like a coyote."

Oct. 4, 1890: Gladys Pyle, who would become the only woman ever to serve the state as a U.S. Senator (1938-39), was born today in Huron. She served as South Dakota Secretary of State, and when Sen. Peter Norbeck died, she was appointed to complete his term.

Oct. 4, 1885: H. L. Brekke started out from Pierre today on what he intended to be a bicycle tour of South Dakota and Minnesota. He peddled as far as nearby Blunt and then changed his plans, taking the train back home to Pierre.

Oct. 4, 1885: Mentor Graham, who was one of Abraham Lincoln's teachers, died today at his home in Blunt.

Oct. 4, 1930: Gov. William Bulow, ill and bedridden at the mansion in Pierre, delivered the dedication address for the Adams Memorial Museum in Deadwood over the telephone.

Oct. 4, 1897: The first automobile was seen on the streets of Aberdeen today.

Oct. 5, 1897: The girls dormitory at the Plankinton Training School burned today, killing seven.

Oct. 5, 1932: Prices on the menu at the grand opening of William Farrell's Coffee Cup Café in Sioux Falls included hamburgers for five cents and pie, ten cents.

Oct. 6, 1874: The Collins-Russell Expedition, including Annie Tallent, secretly left Sioux Falls today bound for the Black Hills, which was then off limits to gold seekers.

Oct. 6, 1941: Daredevil parachutist George Hopkins, 30, of Rapid City, was rescued by eight climbers today from the top of 1,267-foot high Devil's Tower. The ascent took them twelve hours. On Oct. 1, Hopkins had parachuted onto the barren, one-acre top of the tower from an airplane piloted by famed state aviator Clyde Ice.

Daredevil parachutist George Hopkins gained fame in 1941when he landed on the one-acre top of Devil's Tower before figuring out how he would get down. Climbers later rescued him. *Wyoming Commerce Div. Photo*

Oct. 11, 1938: An earthquake jarred buildings, rattled dishes, and caused articles to sway today in Sioux Falls.

Oct. 11, 1899: The Marion Town Council voted today to install a street lamp at the town well.

Oct. 11, 1953: Former Mitchell resident James Earle Fraser, a native of Winona, MN, who would design the buffalo nickel, died today in Westport, CT, at the age of 77.

Oct. 11, 1924: The Yankton to Nebraska Meridian Bridge was dedicated today.

Oct. 13, 1898: Gov. Charles Sheldon, while on a speaking tour in the Black Hills, became ill in Hill City, and eight days later, in Deadwood, he died of pneumonia. Burial was at Pierpont.

Oct. 13, 1942: Joe Foss downed the first of the twenty-six Japanese aircraft he would shoot down during WW II today. Twelve days later, his total bag would be sixteen enemy planes.

Oct. 13, 1899: Peter Anderson's steam thresher engine exploded in a field near Langford, killing four men and leaving the engine a hulk of twisted metal.

Oct. 14, 1964: Billy Mills, an Oglala Sioux, came from behind for a dramatic win in the 10,000 meter race today at the Olympic Games in Tokyo.

Oct. 14, 1899: William McKinley, the first President ever to visit what is now South Dakota, entered the area at Big Stone City today. With four members of his cabinet, the party reviewed the South Dakota Regiment returning from the Spanish-American War, and also visited Watertown, Huron, Sioux Falls, and Yankton while in the state.

Oct. 14, 1907: The government today opened to settlement 56,560 acres of land from the west end of the Lower Brule Reservation a few miles south of Ft. Pierre. There were 3,433 homesteads in the tract, and 4,350 people registered for a chance at the drawing.

Oct. 15, 1877: The first "Deadwood Dick" novel was published by writer Edward Wheeler, who would pen thirty-three Deadwood Dick novels, but never travel further west than Titusville, PA.

Oct. 15, 1880: Owen E. Cotton of Preston Township near Bruce in Brookings County went out during a blizzard to bring his cattle to shelter. Herding them back to his farm, he became disoriented. He held on to the tail of one of the cows and the herd found its way back to the barn. In the barn, he let go of the tail and it snapped off, frozen solid.

Oct. 17, 1924: Sioux Falls residents today dropped a total of $495 into cake pans passed among them as Independent presidential candidate Robert LaFollette stumped the state for support against GOP candidate Calvin Coolidge. It was later discovered that a pick-pocket had wandered through the crowd at the same time, leaving with more money than LaFollette did.

Oct. 20, 1952: Future Major League Baseball player Dave Collins was born today in Rapid City.

Oct. 20, 1894: John West of Tripp was found guilty today of selling diseased meat and was sentenced to six months in jail, where he learned how to break rocks.

Oct. 22, 1924: Canistota's new fire siren was used for the first time today to call volunteer firemen to battle a barn fire on the farm of Mrs. Charles Kostboth.

Oct. 23, 1915: An earthquake in Kadoka caused a loud noise and left cracks in the ground.

Oct. 23, 1940: Over ten thousand people attended the eighth annual State Corn Picking contest on the Roger Kruse farm in Deuel County today. Chance Stone of Deuel County won the contest, picking 28.03 bushels in eighty minutes.

Oct. 25, 1927: Arlene Frame Durkee of Faith, known as the Dakota Nightengale, was chosen to represent South Dakota in a national radio contest sponsored by the Atwater-Kent Foundation. She sang "By The Waters of the Minnetonka" but didn't win.

Oct. 26, 1876: As hoards of grasshoppers were predicted to return in the spring and destroy crops throughout the Midwest, governors of Iowa, Nebraska, Missouri, and Dakota Territory met today in Omaha on the first of a four-day session to discuss what could be done. Among other measures, they recommended fasting and a Day of Prayer, set for May 4, 1877.

Oct. 26, 1909: The first of 81,456 names registered for homestead land near Timber Lake was drawn in Aberdeen today. The first name drawn was Calvin Bowdry of St. Louis, an African American who later filed on land one and one-half miles southeast of Timber Lake.

Oct. 26, 1887: The Sioux Falls Gas Company opened today, but was then destroyed by an explosion that also damaged other property in the vicinity.

Oct. 26, 1886: Cleveland T. Hall, a Civil War veteran who is credited with warning Washington, D.C. of the advance on the city of Confederate General Jubal Early, died today at his Wessington Springs farm home where he homesteaded in 1882.

Oct. 29, 1876: The largest wagon train ever to leave Ft. Pierre headed over the gumbo river breaks for the Black Hills. There were 150 wagons, four hundred men, two women, and five hundred oxen.

Oct. 30, 1941: Ernest Wait, Wessington Springs High School student, died today after a bomb he was making for a Halloween trick exploded in his room. Before he died he was able to tell his mother what the explosive mixture was.

Oct. 30, 1888: The last of four children of Mr. and Mrs. H. M. Hartwell of rural Revillo died today of diphtheria, just seven days after their first child passed away from the disease.

Oct. 31, 1915: A windmill was found standing on Canistota's main street today, left by Halloween pranksters.

Oct. 31, 1862: F. Hayden Carruth, who would become a famous author, was born near Lake City, MN, today. He would later become publisher of the *Estelline* (SD) *Bell* newspaper and in 1911 wrote *Track's End*. He died Jan. 3, 1932.

Oct. 31, 1892: Ft. Randall, after serving as a vital military post for thirty-six years, was closed today.

TUCK'S POST CARD

CARTE POSTALE. _____

POSTKARTE.

(FOR ADDRESS ONLY.)

Mother and Father:
I am working for the furni-
ture store and learning the
embalming business. It is
stressful. Here I am driving
the hearse. Does it look like
me? Homesick, but intend
to stick it out.
Your son
Richard

Mr. Abraham Roth and Wife
RR 3, Box 55

Chapter 23

Stress Test

I had a stress test at the hospital the other day. It was an experience I hope to soon forget.

While the doctor looks on with a concerned expression on his face, the nurses put you on a treadmill set at an angle close to perpendicular, and whip and flog you until you reach warp speed. It's downright criminal the way they urge you on.

Then, as your knees begin to buckle, they unmercifully urge you to go faster for few more minutes. But the tank is empty. It's sorta like pressing harder on the remote control button when you know the batteries in it are dead. It just doesn't do any good.

When you finally do stop, the doctor and nurses retreat to an out-of-the-way corner of the room and study a little computer printout. In hushed voices, you can hear them say things like "my gosh, how old is he anyway?" and "are you sure this is his record?"

They take pictures of your heart with some funny looking Darth Vader-like machine. They look at the pictures, scratch their heads, rub their chins, furrow their brows, and say, "hummm. WOW! Look at that!" Some of them giggle.

All the while, you're trying to decide if it was "Ode to Joy" or "Rock of Ages" you wanted sung at your funeral. But there will be no funeral for a while.

The doctor said I passed, but he urged me to be more serious about my exercising. He said studies have shown that for every mile you jog, you add one minute to your life.

So I'm trying, and so far, based on that study, I figure I will live seven minutes longer than the good Lord originally had planned for me.

I should be pretty good at walking. My mother was a walker. She started when she was sixty. When she turned ninety, we realized we hadn't seen hide nor hair of her for sixteen years. We have no idea where she might be, but we have calculated that if she walked two miles a day for those five thousand days, she'd be somewhere in Asia about now.

She could at least send a postcard.

I'm now walking each day, but the only reason I'm so faithful at it is that it's about the only time I get to hear heavy breathing. I tried jogging out of doors, but the ice cubes jiggled out of my rum and Coke every time I dodged a dog or waved at a friend going the other way.

I decided to join the cadre of mall walkers, but at a mall it's difficult to know if you're coming or going.

So I've pretty well decided to stick with my treadmill, and I've found that walking on it early in the morning works best. My brain doesn't figure out what I'm doing until about 10 a.m. each day, and by then it's too late.

I think I can see some toning up of what used to be my flabby thighs. But I can't be dead certain; it is difficult to see my thighs because of my bulbous stomach sticking out like a sore thumb. I need a full-length mirror.

I remember a few years ago when a friend of mine, a tough old cowboy, told me that if I wanted to live a long life I should sprinkle gunpowder on my bowl of oatmeal every morning. The guy lived to be ninety-three, and I read in his obituary in the paper that when he passed on, he left fourteen children, thirty-two grandchildren, thirty-nine great grandchildren, and a fifteen-foot hole in the wall of the crematorium.

So I switched to cinnamon on my oatmeal the very next day. Like I've always said, old age is when you choose your cereal for the fiber, not the taste.

Some of my buddies are trying to get me to join them at cross country skiing, but if I decided to do that, I'd have to move to a smaller country. I must admit, I do feel better since starting my daily routine on the treadmill.

I urge you to take a stress test. My advice is to wear a thick sweatshirt when you go up to the hospital. It will take the sting out of the cat-o-nine-tails the nurses use to get you going.

By having that test, you'll not only help yourself, but the hospital as well. The treadmill up there is secretly hooked up to a little generator that is then connected to the hospital's electrical system. The wire from the treadmill has been directly hooked into a generator that then is plugged into the hospital's thing-a-ma-jig that looks like a fancy garden hose with a search light, a rotor rooter with a 35 mm panoramic camera on the end, which I have also been privileged to endure.

I think the doctors and nurses call it a sigmoidoscopy.

Now there's an "Ode To Joy," let me tell you.

POST CARD

Place the Stamp here

Mother:
This is old faithful at
Yellowstone. Steam comes out
every now and then, forget the
time. Reminds me of butchering
day on the farm. Except for
sulfer smell. Will start back
tomorrow. We'll be glad to get
back to God's Country.
Nettie

OLD FAITHFUL GEYSER AT SUNRISE—150 FT. YELLOWSTONE PARK.

Chapter 24

Thanksgiving Smells

My childhood memory of Thanksgiving is about turkeys, but it has more to do with my nose and eyes than with my taste buds.

Even now, the smell of wet turkey feathers is etched in my mind, lingering in some fissure in the brain all of these sixty-some years. For the mind's eye, it's the memory of my mother hard at work on an outdoor steam-shrouded turkey picking production line in a rivulet-carved alley behind the creamery in Wessington Springs in 1937.

The steam billowed out of the alley from large, converted oil drums filled with very hot water, sending steam out into a cool November. It carried with it a hint of feathers, wet from the pre-picking dousing each turkey carcass received. The hot bath made the plucking easier.

Steam wafted up in giant clouds out of the alley where the crew, mostly housewives happy to have a part-time job just before Thanksgiving, were preparing Jerauld County birds for the holiday market in Chicago and on east.

For all practical purposes, the Depression was over and money was beginning to flow. Rains had settled down the swirling dust, and crops that fall season had been harvested after several years of no crops at all.

The creamery started up the processing line because birds had to be shipped quickly. Cold storage was something yet to reach the small South Dakota prairie towns. The birds were picked, gutted, packed in barrels with some ice, and quickly loaded onto the afternoon train, which stopped briefly in Wessington Springs almost every day.

So for several days, women of the community earned a post-Depression dime an hour preparing the turkeys for platters back east. The birds waiting their turn were nervous and loud. Their cackling would subside to intermittent clucking as the man moved toward the cage. He reached a strong hand into the top door of the wire pen and grabbed a turkey. Then the raucous cacophony would begin again.

I can't recall now just how each bird was dealt with, but a final blow was administered and the life-blood was drained. Birds thus "processed" were thrown onto a table that resembled a pile of bloody feathers, and my mother and other women would select a handful. Holding the bird by its legs, the turkey was dipped into the drum of hot water, then hung upon brackets for the removal of turkey feathers and the tiny pin-feathers.

My mother was a small woman, less than five feet tall, and she stood on a box so that she could reach the hanging bird. The naked carcasses slid down a pine board made slick from blood and water on the long, makeshift table to other workers who removed the guts. There was a final washing in more drums of hot water, then the birds were packed with ice into wooden barrels for their trip east which would begin that evening at the railroad depot.

I had stopped off at this pre-Thanksgiving production line after school, a few blocks to the north, to see my mother for a reason now long forgotten.

Someone saw me approach, and I heard a call go out for Mae, which was my mother's name. She walked toward me out of a white cloud of smelly steam.

Some of it rolled along with her as she emerged. It was surreal, especially for a first-grader, to see her that way, her hair drooping in a soggy helmet of a hairnet. She wore a too-large rubber apron smeared with blood and small feathers. The apron came down to her ankles.

I have never forgotten the sight of my mother as she appeared magically out of that snow-white cloud of billowing steam. It is etched in my mind's eye still, and each Thanksgiving, it all comes back in living color.

We went to church social last night and herd the Bellmy kids play. They were sure good, but loud. Wish I could do that. We will expect you next month if all goes well. Praying for you.

Rebecca

Herbert Handly
RR 3, Box 55

Chapter 25

Today's Sound

I'm reading this newspaper story about the need for taxpayers to fork over $13,000 so that local barristers can install a sound system in the Brookings County Courthouse.

And I'm wondering why, after nearly a century of lawyers and judges having gotten along in the very same courtroom, there is now this crying-out-loud need for a loudspeaker system.

As I ponder options to cure our now acoustically deficient courtroom, I distinctly hear in the distance what I assume to be a herd of elephants conversing in their low, normally inaudible, throaty rumblings. But there is no marshy waterhole around here that would attract a herd of elephants. In fact, the only elephant in the state that I know of is white and is way down at Vermillion where it is known as the Dakotadome.

The sound I hear and feel in my bones must be the Brookings High School Marching band out on the street practicing. Either the herd or the band is rapidly approaching our place because our cat just hurled a humongous fur ball and is now climbing a wall. Our dishes in the kitchen are rattling, and the newspaper I'm holding begins to shimmy and shake like Mae West with apoplexy.

My wife rushes into the room with an inquisitive look, holding false eyelashes that have mysteriously fallen into her hand. She slips on the fur ball and an eyelash flies off and sticks to a photograph of my mother on the bookcase, landing just below her nose.

The mysterious sound, more a vibration I guess, passes by our house.

Alas, it isn't the marching band or a herd of pachyderms. It's only the neighbor's teenager reporting in, making a final approach to home base in a $4,000 little car wrapped around an $8,000 sound system with an ample load of on-board sub-woofers going full blast and turned to high.

As the automobile that is strapped onto this expensive sound system passes our home, my supper recently devoured is instantly digested in my stomach by the sound waves wafting in from the street.

In our refrigerator, the vibration has zapped some jello into water. Several of our light bulbs pop. My toothpaste tube shrinks to half its size.

and the walnuts in a dish on the table start to do a jerky version of the new dance called the salsa. Our microwave explodes in a puff of black smoke.

Now I know why there is a need for a sound system in the courthouse. We've raised a bunch of hearing deficient teenagers and twenty- and thirty-somethings, once teenagers, who can't hear a whit. The wax in their ears has been turned into stone by their loud music.

Over the past two or three decades, each generation has had to turn the volume knob up another notch to hear the top twenty. Ear drums have left for oblivion.

I remember my days of manual labor as a kid, running the concrete vibrator that jiggled the soupy, just-poured gray mixture into very close proximity to rusty re-bars and oiled wooden forms.

I can't help but picture the brains of these kids who are at ground zero in the music world, sitting right flat-dab next to the expensive vibration machines glowing green and red. The sound waves are settling their little brains in their still-growing craniums right down to about ear level.

So I suppose a $13,000 sound system in the courtroom is needed to provide fair trials for today's miscreants and for the young lawyers and judges who have never heard of Bing Crosby or Teresa Brewer.

Let's bite the bullet, spend the money for the system, and maybe in between trials, we can talk the judge into playing old records by velvet-voiced Mel Torme or Eddie Arnold or somebody.

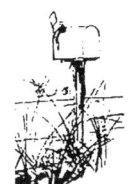

November Postcards

Nov. 2, 1890: Susan B. Anthony was in Deadwood today to help explain the women's suffrage amendment on the eve of the general election vote on the issue, which voters would reject. Twenty-eight years later, in 1918, South Dakotans voted three to one in favor of giving women the right to vote.

Nov. 2, 1889: President Benjamin Harrison signed documents today that made South Dakota and North Dakota the thirty-ninth and fortieth states, but the president intentionally shuffled the two proclamations so it is not known which was the first of the two to gain statehood.

Nov. 3, 1892: A threshing machine steam traction engine exploded today near Redfield, killing several men and a fifteen-year-old boy, Edwin Hickey of near Chamberlain. He became the first child buried in Lyman County.

Nov. 3, 1936: The majority of voters in Brookings, Turner, Lake, Lincoln, Kingsbury, Hamlin, and Deuel Counties cast their ballots for Alf Landon over Franklin D. Roosevelt, who won in all other South Dakota counties.

Nov. 4, 1925: An unusual egg contest that started last spring and ended the last day of October in Bruce was won by Leo Cotton, who brought 16,668 eggs to the Goff Store from his hen house. He won one hundred pounds of sugar.

Nov. 7, 1929: The Eden Bank was robbed today by two armed men who took $3,000.

Nov. 7, 1883: The town of LaFoon was voted as the Faulk County seat, but the victory was short-lived. So was LaFoon.

Nov. 8, 1923: Four armed men left after robbing the First National Bank of Groton, but shots from Pete Kourkulas as they departed injured one, who dropped $58,000 in bonds and $3,847 in cash and gold as he felt the bullet. The men got away, but with only $813.

Nov. 8, 1958: Edwin Johnson, early Elk Point area farmer and inventor of the revolving chicken de-header machine and other devices, died today.

Nov. 8, 1932: FDR got 64.1 percent of the South Dakota vote in the general election, and Herbert Hoover garnered 35.9 percent. In all, 282,727 South Dakotans cast ballots.

Nov. 8, 1950: A future Miss America runner-up, Mary Johanna Harum, aka Mary Hart, was born today. She taught English in the Sioux Falls school system and later gained fame as a television show host.

Nov. 8, 1923: *The Groton Independent* newspaper today reported on a New York feature article on local jockey Earl Sande, who had just ridden Zev to victory in an international match at Belmont Race Track.

Nov. 10, 1885: Charles Coughlin, who would later donate funds to build the landmark Campanile on the State University campus in Brookings, was born today in Carthage.

Nov. 11, 1918: An effigy of the German Kaiser was burned on Deadwood's main street today.

Nov. 11, 1887: William L. McKnight was born in a sod hut near White today. He would become president of 3M Company in 1925 and its board chairman in 1949.

Nov. 11, 1870: A jury in Vermillion today found Pvt. William Barry of the 13th U.S. Infantry innocent of killing English officer Wilfred Speers on June 8, 1867, on the steamboat *Octavia* while it cruised the Missouri in what would become North Dakota. The case caused an international furor.

Nov. 11, 1936: A balloon measuring 315 feet high carried Army Air Corps officers Orville Anderson and Albert Stevens, both wearing football helmets inside Explorer II, to 13.71 miles above sea level out of the Stratobowl in the Black Hills. The balloon and pod weighed 7.5 tons. It landed near White Lake, SD, 230 miles away eight hours after launch. The altitude record stood for twenty-one years.

Nov. 11, 1946: George McPherson, who brought the first purebred Hereford cattle to the West River country from Menlo, IA, in 1883, died today in Meade County.

Nov. 11, 1889: The cornerstone of the State Soldiers Home in Hot Springs was laid today.

Nov. 11, 1934: The most severe dust storm ever billowed and rolled into Aberdeen.

Nov. 12, 1885: The now ghost town of Diana in Sanborn County was struck by fire and the town's covered skating rink and Ed Patterson's home and shop were destroyed. Townspeople raised $100 for Patterson to rebuild.

Nov. 12, 1934: A dust storm dubbed a black blizzard brought visibility in Presho this Sunday down to almost zero. And a severe dust storm rolled over Jerauld County at 8:30 a.m., carried by winds of sixty miles an hour. Lights in homes had to be turned on during most of the day because the cloud blotted out the sun.

Nov. 12, 1924: The bridge over the Missouri River at Mobridge was dedicated today.

Nov. 12, 1929: An explosion shortly after midnight today blew out the front of the Bank of Norden at Lake Norden, and the three burglars walked down the middle of the street with the swag in a flour sack. They made their escape but were later captured. Two served in the penitentiary and one got off on a technicality. All three were later killed attempting to rob a bank in another state.

Nov. 15, 1815: John Banvard, artist and poet who gained fame and fortune by painting a panorama of the Mississippi River that measured three miles long, depicting 1,200 miles of river shoreline, was born today in New York. On opening night of showing the panorama in Louisville, KY, no one came, but the unique show with the long canvas rolled from one side of the stage to another like a large scroll, did gain acceptance and become very popular. Banvard came to Watertown, SD, in 1884 and died there in 1891.

Nov. 16, 1909: Emil Victor today became the first person legally hanged in Aberdeen for the murder of the Christie Family and Michael Ronayne near Rudolph, SD.

Nov. 18, 1915: Sixteen Mitchell bachelors who called themselves the Mitchell Comrades of '79 after they all survived the 1879-80 blizzard, met today in Firesteel for a reunion.

Nov. 26, 1964: The National Falconry Convention began today in Centerville.

Nov. 26, 1931: Laura Ingalls Wilder learned today that her first book, *The Little House In The Big Woods*, had been accepted for publication.

POST CARD

Place the Stamp here

CENT
States
ssessions
ada and
ICO
ENTS
reign

I finally found a job out here. I am
working on Mt. Rushmore this
summer, cooking for the men. Long
hours, but beautiful here. Saw
mountain goats yesterday.
Love and XXXXXX
Betsy
P.S—It gets cold out here at night,
but warms up during the day. Noisy
when they blast the faces.

9300

The Harold Smiths
RR 4, Box 2

VIEW FROM
SHEEP MOUNTAIN
RISE STUDIO
RAPID CITY
S. D.

Chapter 26

Punished Womans Goat Man

One of my first feature stories as a young reporter for the *Watertown* (SD) *Public Opinion* was about the Punished Womans Goat Man. I often think of that story and the man it was about. I have written thousands of stories about South Dakotans through the years, but that story was always one of my favorites.

I had a general idea where the Goat Man lived, and drove my car as close to the site as possible, then got out and walked into the brush in hopes I could find him. He was there, amidst a small, junky yard filled with old washers, dryers, and refrigerator carcasses. The Goat Man, John Freund, was suspicious of me at first. But he soon warmed to my presence as we visited for about an hour. I leaned against one of the old, discarded washing machines he had moved to his front yard from the nearby South Shore dump grounds. He sat on a wooden box and leaned on his cane.

John was a small, thin man with a whirlwind beard. Despite the warmth of the day, he wore a sweater beneath his shirt, the top of which was held close around his neck by a safety pin. His bib overalls, too, were patched with safety pins holding together small rips in the fabric. He poked the dirt around him with his cane as he talked. Curiously, he wore plastic bags as stockings, and his shoes didn't match. One, obviously too small for his right foot, had been split and expanded. A thin strip of cloth was tied around one pant leg like a bicycle clip.

Old equipment such as washing machines and other throw-aways formed a fence of sorts to keep his herd of goats in check and to mark his territory. He felt intruders were lurking nearby at night intending to kill his goats.

Here John Freund's story, as published in the *Public Opinion* on June 24, 1961:

John Freund, who says he must be "somewhere around 80," lives in a cave on the shores of Punished Womans Lake.

"I like to live alone," he said. "My goats keep me company," Freund explained, pointing to four frisky animals chained to stakes near his dug-out home on a small, 15-acre plot of land just east of South Shore in Codington County.

He said that looking after his goats required considerable work, and that he spent most of the rest of the time reading his vast supply of religious material.

"I'm Catholic, but there is no church here and I can't walk as far as I used to be able to, so I get my religion from books," said Freund, who never got further than halfway through the first reader in grade school. He never married.

Freund's life for about the past 30 years has been that of a recluse, but it hasn't been because he doesn't like people. He'll talk your leg off on any subject from goats to Ghana.

He said that for most of the more than 30 years ("I'm not sure, you lose track of time when you live alone."), that he's been living alone and liking it, he hasn't eaten a cooked meal.

He's a vegetarian and because of the danger of fire and because someone usually steals parts of his stoves, he doesn't cook his food. "My favorite is raw, uncooked oatmeal covered with chocolate syrup and some goat milk," he said, explaining that he usually eats that dish twice each day. "Sometimes I get busy around here and forget to eat at all."

Freund said that lately, he's been trying out cold canned goods.

He doesn't use a heating stove in his dugout, either. But somehow, he makes it through the cold winters without contracting so much as a cold.

"If I do happen to come down with something, I take a pinch of Epsom salts like I have here," he said, pulling a small green bottle out of a pocket of his patched overalls. "If you ever get sick," he said, "a touch of Epsom salts will make you feel fit as a fiddle."

He added that the salt also works wonders for sick goats, and said that if the Epsom salt didn't work, aspirin would.

Freund's preference for not using a stove caused some concern a few years ago with members of the state welfare office. When he applied for old age assis-

Recluse John Freund sought the peace and quiet of Punished Womans Lake near South Shore in Codington County and carved and shoveled a dugout home on the lake's shore. He kept goats with him for warmth in the winter. *Chuck Cecil Photo*

tance, he told the county office that he did not need funds for fuel because he did not use a stove.

That's the way his application was sent on to Pierre. It wasn't long before the state officials were calling the county office to remind them of the "mistake."

No mistake, Pierre was told, the man simply does not use a stove for either cooking or heating. Pierre officials learned that Freund kept his goats in his dugout café during the cold months, sleeping on a straw-filled bunk over the animals, getting needed warmth from them. He covered himself with burlap and an old army trench coat, he said.

But state officials knew that federal inspectors would never believe the story of Freund's winter habit, so decided to include in his allotment something for fuel, which he now uses for food for his goats, which are, in fact, his cave's heat supply.

Freund was born on a farm near Waverly. He worked on the farm for several years, then went to work for the railroad and also worked part time in a Waverly store.

"When I enrolled in grade school I was about 12 years old," he recalled. "The teacher put me in a grade with six-year-olds and I didn't like that very much."

He said that when he decided to leave school he didn't really know how to read. "I didn't even know my multiplication tables, either."

Later, he worked for a farmer who had a large chest full of books. He was given permission to browse through the chest, which he did, eventually learning how to read. Freund came to Watertown in about 1925 and worked for a time as an elevator operator in the Lincoln Hotel. While in Watertown, he lived in an abandoned railroad boxcar in the southeast section of town.

"I had a stove that I used outside," he recalled, "but people kept stealing parts from it. Then I tried using a small barrel to build a fire in, and then I decided to forget about cooking and heating my home," he said.

"But I did insulate the boxcar. I used cardboard mattress boxes both inside and out and put tin over the cardboard on the outside. It was warm inside. Sometimes the water froze, but I was used to it and it didn't bother me."

Freund said he decided to move from Watertown after several of the goats he kept were shot or killed in some other manner. He moved to his present home in South Shore in about 1945.

"It took me only about two weeks to dig my dugout," he said. At the time, he was 65. Freund said he was happy in South Shore, but still had trouble keeping his goats alive. "But Watertown is a bigger goat hating town," he said.

"I like it here, I've got all my teeth and I'm hardly ever sick," he said, adding that he is concerned about one thing. "Whenever I go into a store in town during the cold weather it's so hot inside that I get dizzy and have to sit down for a while."

* * *

It was a slow, cold day for news at the *Public Opinion* about a year later. Afternoons after the paper came out were quiet times in the news room, with the only distraction being the clattering teletype machines typing out-of-state and national news. The telephone rang and I answered. It was the funeral home calling to tell me of a death, and passing along the funeral and information so I could write an obituary for John Freund of South Shore.

The funeral director said that law enforcement authorities had called him after Mr. Freund's body was discovered. I took the obituary information and then, out of curiosity, called the Codington County Sheriff. He told me that he had been notified by a South Shore shop keeper who became concerned because of the blizzard that had just passed through the area that week.

Freund had last been seen on Saturday when he came into town for supplies. A blizzard roared over South Shore the following Monday, Tuesday, and Wednesday. It was a particularly bad storm, with no travel advised and visibility at times down to zero as the wind sent snow skittering across the fields and down the streets of South Shore. Because of the intensity of the storm, two men in town, after the storm passed, decided to check on Mr. Freund.

The sheriff said they went to Freund's lakeside cave and called for Freund, but got no answer. They could hear goats bleating inside the cave, but were unable to force open the wooden door that Freund had crafted from driftwood that had washed up on the shore nearby. By this time, his small goat herd had grown to about thirty animals, the sheriff said. The men were finally able to force open the door a few inches so that they could see inside.

Freund had apparently realized something was wrong, perhaps another dizzy spell came on, and he had made his way to the cave door. There, he sat down with his back against the old wooden door and died. It was during the cold of winter and within hours his body had frozen solid in the seated position, which explained why the men could not easily open the door. The goats were nearly starved but survived by eating the straw from Freund's bed and oatmeal from the sack on a shelf in the cave, plus other items having some faint nutritional value. Hungry rats, however, had found Freund's body, the sheriff told me.

Mr. Freund's obituary indicated that he was born March 8, 1884. When I asked him that question during our interview a year earlier, he told me he wasn't sure of the exact date.

He is buried in the St. Joseph Catholic Church Cemetery in Waverly.

POST CARD

GILBERT

Dear Aunt Grace.
You would enjoy the Black
Hills and your rock collection
would grow. I'll bring one
back for you.
Love
Niece Janice

Mrs. Grace Jones
J&L Ranch

Chapter 27

Arco, Minnesota

Tiny Arco, just across the Brookings County border in Lincoln County, may be losing population, but it has a permanent collection of carefully arranged rocks for all ages.

The rocks hail from every state in the union and were artfully cemented in worldly order over fifty years ago by members of the talented H. P. Pedersen family. Some of their then-famous rock garden remains today a block from the town's old creamery building, now a steak house, in this little prairie community of one hundred.

"It was really something in its day," recalled retired Arco Postmaster Stanley Ostergaard, who now lives in nearby Ivanhoe ten miles north of Arco. He gets back to his hometown regularly to meet old buddies and play cards in the town's main street restaurant, which is closed. "We all have keys, so we go in, make a pot of coffee, and play cards once a week," he said.

When Ostergaard was postmaster, he lived across the street from the Arco Texaco Station where the Pedersen family created a castle-like structure out of a mundane filling station. Around the station, they created a unique garden of rock with rock sculptures of all shapes and sizes.

"Whenever the Pedersen family took a trip they always had a little two-wheel trailer behind the car and they collected rocks from all over the country," Ostergaard remembered.

In the 1940s and early 1950s, Arco was a mecca of sorts to persons who had heard of the famous Arco rock garden. Thousands of people traveling through the area stopped to see the wonders the Pedersens created. Few travelers stop in Arco now, but remnants of the famous garden of rock still remain.

The sculptured rock garden was started in the 1930s when H. P. and Ricka Pedersen took an interest in collecting rocks. Soon, with an ample supply of rocks hauled back home on their little trailer, they decided to begin building homemade objects people might buy, such as ashtrays, lamps, flower pots, and book ends.

Each object started as a chicken-wire frame, and small rock mosaics were added to the mortar surrounding the frames. Their creations sold well.

Dave Herzog and Lez Norling outside their unusual home in Arco, MN. The home was once a Texaco gas station gradually transformed by the stone work of Mr. and Mrs. H. P. Pedersen, who once owned the station. The circles of stone atop the building once had stone Texaco stars hanging inside them. *Chuck Cecil Photo*

"They spent countless hours building them," recalled granddaughter Mrs. Jean Stefansen of Tyler, MN. "They couldn't keep up with demand," she said. "They must have crushed thousands of rocks. They found some of them when they traveled to the Black Hills or other places."

"It got to the point where neighbors started to save unusual rocks for them," Stefansen remembered.

Soon, the Pedersen sons Vernon and M.M. got interested and started helping in the project, learning the rudiments of rock sculpting as they watched their parents at work.

It was during the last year of the Dust Bowl and drought in the area, 1936, that H. P. Pedersen purchased the Arco Service Station. During slow times at the station, he came up with a money-making idea for rocks. While he and Ricka continued to make and sell their small household rock creations, they also began to make large rock sculptures displayed around the old corner filling station. "Bus loads of people would come to see that rock garden," Mrs. Stefansen said. Family records show that in 1949, over 4,000 people visited the filling station and garden.

The station soon took on a castle-like façade, and in the side yard, more and more sculptures were added. These included a wide variety of rock sculptures, from a miniature stone farmstead to a large Viking ship with billowing sails made of rock. If there is a theme of the building's façade, it is of outer space. The gasoline station sold Texaco brand products and the company's logo on each gas pump was a star.

The Pedersens duplicated this star logo on the front roofline of the station. Five old automobile iron tire rims covered with small rocks formed the frame from which were hung sturdy five-pointed Texaco stars made of rock. The Texaco logo was also incorporated into a large, colorful star over the station's entry. The station was closed long ago, and it has now been refurbished and is the comfortable home of Dave Herzog, a local trucker.

"The iron bolts holding the stars in place were rusting so we took the stars down for safety's sake," said Herzog.

The Pedersens used rocks of every kind, from coral to rose quartz, Sioux quartzite, pipestone, and petrified wood, among others, to form the façade.

As the filling station itself took on its new layer of rock, the rock garden on the station's east side continued to grow. Before the family was finished, there were pelicans, a life-sized goat named Hugo, a large pheasant, a windmill, a large snake wound around a large petrified log, and a working lighthouse, among many other objects.

This sculpture of a goat made of stone collected by Mr. and Mrs. H. P. Pedersen of Arco, MN, in Lincoln County near South Dakota's Brookings County is one of several still remaining from the once thriving menagerie of the Pedersens. *Chuck Cecil Photo*

H. P. Pedersen died in 1942. His son Vernon, when he returned from WW II service in 1946, took up the cudgel and continued the creative work at the station.

Among Vernon's most famous additions was a one thousand-pound, seven-foot high Statue of Liberty. A light was placed in the statue's torch which was turned on at night. Vernon told his sister that the statue required over two hundred hours of labor to build.

In 1952, he sold the station and took some of the rock garden's objects with him to Clarissa, MN, north of Alexandria.

But the elaborately decorated filling station remained and Herzog, the current occupant, enjoys living in the unusual house. "We've covered most of the rock on the inside with paneling, but the mop boards and the window casings in the front part of the house are of rock embedded in cement," says

Herzog. The home also has an adjacent tool shed, the only round, rock tool shed in the county.

Although passersby seldom stop or come to the door for a closer inspection of the unusual house, "lots of people drive by slowly to take a good look," Herzog said.

Some of the minute detail the Pedersens incorporated in their sculptured façade requires close inspection. Below the window sills, for example, are tiny likenesses of animals carved from pipestone. An apple-sized round rock has a stem carved from pipestone.

A large garage now covers the land where most of the extensive rock garden once stood. But four of the Pedersen rock sculptures have been saved by Arco residents. The statues have been moved to the camping and recreation area along nearby Lake Stay.

The Statue of Liberty, a liberty bell, and Hugo the mountain goat are there, standing as silent reminders next to an elaborate stone wall which once set off the famous Arco Rock Garden.

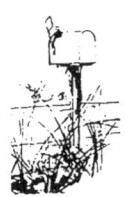

December Postcards

Dec. 2, 1850: Caton Hoblit was born today. He became a Clark County rancher and is remembered for his size. He weighed 512 pounds. He was so large that he required a special slide and pulley arrangement to get to and from his bed to a reinforced buggy parked beneath a first floor window at his ranch home. In the buggy, he had rigged a threshing machine power belt from one side of the buggy to the other, which supported his huge stomach when he bumped along to town in the buggy. In Clark, he had his lunch delivered to him while he sat immobile in his buggy.

Dec. 2, 1951: Charles Nordin of Stanley County, who built the fireplace in the Governor's Mansion, died today in Deadwood.

Dec. 5, 1976: One of the rodeo world's most famous bucking horses, Tipperary, was inducted into the Oklahoma City Rodeo Hall of Fame today. A monument in his memory stands in Buffalo, SD, where he is buried.

Dec. 7, 1885: Kimball's efforts for a city well were successful at 1,068 feet when drillers hit an artesian layer and a column of water eight inches in diameter shot sixteen feet into the air. Farmers who later came to Kimball from miles around for water said it was easier to drive into Kimball for water than it would be to drill for it on their farmsteads.

Early Clark County rancher Caton Hoblit, who grew so large that he had to be lifted by block and tackle from his bed and slid out the bedroom window on a heavy board onto his reinforced buggy, which he used to manage his ranch and make trips into nearby Clark for supplies. In Clark, he would order meals from a local café and eat them while still sitting in the buggy. *Submitted Photo*

Dec. 7, 1900: Earl Thode was born today near Belvidere. In 1939 he became the first champion bronc rider and all-around cowboy named under a new plan of consolidated point ratings instituted by the Rodeo Association of America.

Dec. 8, 1856: The man who would one day operate the largest ranch in South Dakota, Harry Oelrichs, was born today in Baltimore, MD. Oelrichs, after whom the town of Oelrichs is named, served as president of the Anglo American Cattle Company when it was organized with eastern money in 1880. A packing plant was built on the ranch that operated until 1888. In its heyday the ranch employed hundreds of cowboys and had a remuda of over one thousand cow ponies.

Dec. 9, 1947: Tom Daschle, who would become Senate Majority Leader in the early twenty-first century, was born today in Aberdeen. He was the first South Dakotan ever elected to that high Senate position by his peers.

Dec. 9, 1908: Hump, a Minneconju Sioux chief, died today at Cherry Creek at age 60. One year to the day later, Chief Swift Bear also died, as did Chief Red Cloud, in his Pine Ridge home.

A young Tom Daschle discusses an issue with the late Wisconsin Sen. William Proxmire.

Dec. 11, 1904: Marian Antoinette Kalayjian, world-famous pianist of the late 1920s and 30s, was born today in Parker.

Dec. 11, 1943: The most disastrous airplane crash to date in South Dakota happened thirteen miles west of Mission, killing all ten Air Force men on a B-17F training mission out of Ellsworth AFB, Rapid City.

Dec. 13, 1962: Harriet Horning of Watertown, the first woman ever elected SD Secretary of State, died today in Watertown of cancer.

Dec. 13, 1913: South Dakota wrestling champion Olaf Karp of Viborg was defeated tonight by Iowan John Hessen. After fifty-two minutes of fighting, Hessen got a fall using a toe hold.

Dec. 14, 1942: A practice blackout drill darkened South Dakota as the nation prepared for WWII with Japan. It was the first time lights over the entire state had ever been turned off at the same time.

Dec. 14, 1892: Hard up for news to fill the *White Chief*, George Chase wrote in his newspaper: "Don't forget that the editor wants all the news. If your wife gives you a licking or runs away or if you are sick or anything happens that is of interest, you will confer a favor upon the public by letting us know."

Dec. 15, 1890: Sitting Bull, 59, was killed today at Bullhead Village near Mobridge by Indian Police.

Dec. 15, 1935: The first of what would be seventeen days of snowfall began today, and on Jan. 1, 1936, high winds added to the problem, creating one of the worst ever blizzards in the state.

Dec. 15, 1882: James L. Gilmore, a mule skinner on the Deadwood Trail who shot and killed Bicente Ortez about fifty miles out of Ft. Pierre in June of 1879, was legally hanged today in Deadwood. Mexican Creek in Haakon County is named in honor of Ortez.

Dec. 16, 1930: Citizens in Wessington Springs voted 394 to 278 against allowing movies to be shown on Sundays. Six elections on the question would take place over the next eleven years until movies on Sundays were approved in a 1941 vote.

Dec. 18, 1923: The temperature in Mellette in Spink County reached ninety-two degrees today, and residents gathered in swim suits at the William Cliff home for croquet and ice cream.

Dec. 24, 1879: Ole and Kersti Fossum of Minneahaha County lost a son who was eight months old and another son ten years old today to a diphtheria epidemic. Two days before, their six-year-old son died of the disease.

Dec. 25, 1876: An African American named W. T. Archery became the first recorded death in Deadwood today. He passed away in his cabin of natural causes.

Dec. 25, 1941: Robert Hedman, a native of Webster, became the first flying ace of WW II when he shot down five enemy planes in thirty minutes over Rangoon, Burma, where he flew for Gen. Claire Chennault as a Flying Tiger.

Dec. 26, 1914: Movie star Richard Widmark, who lived as a youngster in Sioux Falls, was born today in Sunrise, MN.

Dec. 29, 1890: The Chicago and North Western Railroad reached Deadwood today.

Dec. 29, 1890: The Massacre at Wounded Knee took place today at the hands of Gen. Nelson A. Miles and 7th Cavalry troopers escorting Big Foot and his band back to the reservation. Thirty-one soldiers and 150 Indians died in what would be the last major conflict between the Indians and the government.

Dec. 31, 1901: Robert Ames shot Frank Handley on the Handley Ranch northwest of Presho in the early morning today. Ames was sentenced to twenty years in prison, but escaped. He was later captured and given a life sentence.

Dec. 31, 1936: Criminals intending to eliminate two gang members placed them in the Larson Hardware Powder House seven miles east of Sioux Falls today. They ignited the house, and the four tons of blasting powder and one and one-half tons of dynamite left a crater twenty-five feet deep. It is said windows were broken in nearby Dell Rapids and Canton. Although shot and near death, one of the two gang members was able to escape before the blast and lived to tell the tale.

Dec. 31, 1927: Engineer Lou Baschky and Fireman Frank Brown died in a Bullington train crash after the train careened brakeless from the top of Whitewood summit near Nemo enroute to Deadwood. Two other crewmen jumped to safety, but Baschky and Brown courageously stuck with the runaway to the end.

TUCK'S POST CARD

CARTE POSTALE.   POSTKARTE.

(FOR ADDRESS ONLY.)

Dear Mom and Pa
     Dad's folks are doing
fine, living near us and we
check on them everyday.
Don't worry. They are fine.
Grandpa still milks his cow.
Grandma made a pie today.
Weather good.
John

Mr. and Mrs. Jack Yonkoseth
RR 3, Box 32
Br

Chapter 28

Hetland Blacksmith

Dale Andersen's big blacksmith hands are still helping shape history in his hometown of Hetland.

But at 88, nursing a bad back and retired after nearly seventy-five years of sharpening plow lathes, pinching red-hot iron rims on wooden wagon wheels, and repairing all kinds of farm and home equipment, his involvement in the activities of this Kingsbury community of fifty has changed.

The long-time village smithy, town home run baseball slugger, occasional preacher, former school board member, and town trustee is known as "Mory" after his father Morris, who was the village blacksmith here before his son took over.

Hands that once shaped big iron over a red-hot forge now fashion dainty, delicious loaves of homemade bread that he makes and bakes as

Blacksmith Dale Andersen of Hetland with the big hammer his father gave him when he started working summers at the shop at the age of 14. The workbench and tool rack are exactly as Dale left them when he retired over a dozen years ago. *Chuck Cecil Photo*

a hobby. He happily gives them away to friends and passersby. Helping others is another hobby he pursues.

For example, he's taken it upon himself to mow the lawns of other Hetland senior citizens and to keep the weeds down on the city's public property. "To keep the town looking nice," he says. "I'm on my third lawnmower and sixth bread maker."

Mory would rather be working on plow lathes (some call them lays), than putting up with his back, which now protests decades of horsing around heavy iron in his now-locked blacksmith shop across the street from his home, with its porch full of cats, foreign and domestic, that gather there for free handouts, and to sleep in the sun on a carpeted porch step.

When he can, he still works with iron, making decorative items from old, square nails and iron horseshoes scrounged from piles in his rusting, cluttered shop, one of the last blacksmith shops left in these parts.

For that matter, Mory is probably one of the state's last living blacksmiths from the age of horse-drawn farm machinery which passed slowly from the South Dakota scene after WW II.

Andersen's father, Morris, arrived in America from Thisted, Denmark, in 1899. He settled in Hetland four years later and fired up his blacksmith forge that is still in the old Hetland shop. Morris soon bought out his competition, the shop then owned by L. W. Barber, and skidded the old Barber building that even today is the old Andersen Blacksmith Shop, across the street.

And that's where Dale, his son, picked up his father's practice and carried on the blacksmith tradition for nearly seventy-five years, until the demand for blacksmith work dwindled to a trickle and forced him to close the doors for good.

In that old wood-frame building, its front covered with pressed-tin siding over interior walls blackened by decades of forge smoke and cyanide fumes, Andersen went to work in the summer of 1928 at the age of 14.

Before being given a real job by his father, he spent all the time he could at the shop, watching the skillful iron work, fascinated—and warmed in the winter—by the hot forge fire. He remembers the arcing sparks flying from the anvil at every clang of a big hammer in his father's huge hands.

On a tour of his shop, the metal tools and machines rusting from misuse, Andersen found an old hammer that his father had given him on his first day of work in 1928. He tried it out and threw it back on the bench where it clanged in a dusty landing on a pile of other hand tools once used to bend and tame steel.

With his cane, he pointed to where the forge had been and affectionately tapped a rusting metal cutter older than he is. He stopped to

Dale is the son of blacksmith Mory Andersen, and the old shop where both worked still stands, although silent now, the forge fire doused when Dale retired years ago. Note the sign over the door. *Chuck Cecil Photo*

inspect a window behind an iron grill his father attached to the window frame from scrap iron, to protect the glass from the heavy hooves and wide rumps of nervous workhorses brought to town for new shoes.

Andersen's first jobs as a boy of 14 included sharpening and straightening plow shares, or lathes, which were the tough metal strips on the bottom of the plow's curved moldboard. "We were known as the best place around for fixing plow lays," he said. "Farmers from as far away as Minnesota brought their lays to us."

He remembered one day when he and his dad counted six hundred lathes waiting in the shop to be fixed, more than two hundred outside on the ground waiting their turn inside, and three hundred more in the back room finished and ready for the farmers to pick up on their next trip to Hetland. "You couldn't hardly walk around in there for plow lays," he said.

Andersen learned early how to remove and straighten the lathes' dings and dents caused by collisions with field stones. He explained that the lathes were heated and then he used the heavy trip hammer to smooth the steel. Then, the lathes were sprinkled with cyanide while still red-hot. He said the cyanide made the lathe "scour (the soil) better." And he remembered the fumes from the cyanide. "They would just roll up off the lathes." He recalled that on a visit to see a doctor, who took an X-ray of his chest, the physician asked if he was a coal miner "because my lungs were so black from those fumes."

The final treatment for the lathe after the cyanide bath was a second bath in a large tank of salt water to further harden the steel. "We'd dump salt into the tank until an egg would float," he said, "then we knew we had enough salt to do the job right."

Andersen said he has always loved blacksmithing. There was never any doubt about what he wanted to do after graduation from Hetland High School. He had an appointment to the Naval Academy, but that didn't work out at the last minute, and soon after, he started working full-time at his father's shop.

During those early years learning the business, Andersen, like most other blacksmiths, was literally branded into the profession. In Andersen's case, his brand came from a red-hot wagon rim that fell, landing on his arm and leaving a thick scar still visible just above his wrist. He wears it as a badge of blacksmithing honor.

"Oh, sure, you burned your hands a lot and got sparks down your neck all the time, but that was just part of the territory," he said. In blacksmithing's heyday, there was enough business at the Andersen and Son shop to provide a good living for both Dale and his dad.

"We charged a dollar to shrink a wagon rim and seventy-five cents to shrink on a new buggy rim," he recalled. The need for new iron rims was because the wooden tires would dry out and shrink over time, and the factory applied steel rim would fall off.

So the steel rim was cut down and re-welded, then while still red-hot, forced over the wooden rim to insure a snug marriage of wood and steel. "We did a lot of that kind of work," Andersen said.

In between work sharpening lathes and re-fitting wagon wheels, Andersen and his father in the 1930s invented an unusual and admit-

Retired Hetland SD blacksmith Dale Andersen, 88, inspects the homemade tractor he and his father named Hitler that they made during slack times at the shop during WW II. Behind Andersen is a duck hunting boat he made and used once. It didn't float. *Chuck Cecil Photo*

tedly ungainly lawn mower prototype. It was fine tuned, and once the bugs were worked out, the Andersens began producing them for residents at $75 a machine.

Power was from old airplane starters which were connected to a pulley attached to Model T Ford water pumps that turned a twenty-four-inch blade. Wheels were from discarded bicycles. Once, the Andersens even tried wheels off an old wheelchair. The mowers sold well, but soon factory models started showing up in catalogs and at hardware stores. "We should have gotten a patent on that thing," Dale said, "but we didn't know any better, I guess."

During WW II, with three of Dale's older brothers off to war, he and his father crafted an old tractor that they figured the Andersen boys could use on farms after they returned from the war.

They christened their creative contraption "Hitler," after Adolph Hitler, the Nazi dictator. "Hitler" was made from an old Fordson tractor. The rear axel, transmission, and wheels were tipped upside down and mounted on a frame to give the machine more ground clearance. An old Nash automobile motor powered the tractor.

"It did a good job and would run all day on five gallons of gas," Dale remembered. It is still there, out behind the shop in Hetland in 2002, rusting away, as small shoots from a nearby elm tree grow up between its framing.

After WW II, the demand for good blacksmiths diminished because of better built, bigger farm machinery, but now alone in the shop, Dale's talents for fixing big steel continued to be in demand up into the 1980s. "But those last years were tough years," he remembered. He left the shop and tried selling insurance part-time, then retired altogether in 1999, one of the last of South Dakota's venerable blacksmiths to hang up the forge tongs.

Nov 17, 1906.

Well we were out taking in the sights of the City to day. it was very rainy day. So we had a few of these taken for the fun of it. Has been very disagreeable weather so far. Suppose you all know who these are. Best Regards from the Family!

Fishback Home

Age has not dulled the elegance and beauty of the 101-year-old Fishback home in Brookings.

It still stands, sedate and statuesque, a reminder of times past, competing on more than even terms with the newer homes of today.

It's a museum quality example of home and family life of another era. But it is still lived in. The current occupants, Van and Barbara Fishback, are working to keep it fit for today while mindful of the family joy and comfort it brought to Van's parents and grandparents.

Fishback said that he and his wife hope to continue to improve the home and restore it to near its original condition. "It's exciting for us to prepare the house for its second century of use, whatever that might be," he said.

The Greek-pillared structure was built in 1902 and has always been occupied by members of the Fishback family. Set back from the residential street on about two acres of manicured lawns, the big white house appears as if from a *Gone With The Wind* movie set.

The Fishback home in Brookings was constructed in 1902 by the Horace Fishback, Sr. family, and has remained in the Fishback family since. It is now occupied by Van and Barbara Fishback. Van is the grandson of Horace Sr. Note the canopy carriage entry on the side of the house. The home has 7,553 square feet of space and is of neoclassic design. *Chuck Cecil Photo*

This is the music room in the Fishback home. Note the stencil designs on the ceiling. Walls in this room are covered in silk. *Chuck Cecil Photo*

Three generations of Fishbacks have called the three-story, 7,553-square foot building home. Furniture pieces in the home were there when the family of Horace Fishback Sr. moved in nearly 101 years ago. He was instrumental in starting what is today the First National Bank in Brookings. The bank is under the leadership of Horace Sr.'s grandsons, Robert and Van Fishback.

Their parents, the late Margaret and Horace Jr. moved into the home in 1939 and raised Robert, Van, and three other children there.

The house is of neoclassic design, says Dr. Edward Hogan, author of the book *South Dakota House Types*, and associate vice president of academic affairs at South Dakota State University.

"That type of home was built in the early days to look like a government building," Hogan said. "It has impressive arches, columns, and things like impressive window dormers," he said.

Greeting visitors near the front door is a magnificent grandfather clock, which has been chiming out the hours in the home for a century. It reaches nearly to the eleven-foot ceilings.

To the left of the entry, off a wide foyer, is a music room that was once a popular gathering spot for family members and guests for card games and caroms, or music on the beautiful Steinway piano. The brightly-lit room still has its original silk wall covering and some of the original furniture.

Daryl Petersen, who as a boy growing up in Brookings in the 1940s helped his father and uncle, local painters Valde and Carl, repair ceiling stenciling in the Fishback house in 2002. He was asked to help make further repairs to the stenciled ceiling in the living room. He used his father's stenciling tools and brushes. *Chuck Cecil Photo*

Lining the doorway to the music room are the original portieres, or velvet curtains, which can be drawn to close off the room.

The living room features a huge fireplace over ten feet high. It is one of three fireplaces in the house. To finish the fireplace and much of the woodwork, skilled craftsmen from St. Paul, MN, came to Brookings for this finishing touch. While in town, they lived in tents in the pasture behind the home, now a developed residential area. The finish on the fireplaces and the woodwork remains today what they so skillfully applied over a century ago. It has never been refurbished or touched except for light dusting.

The ceiling in this room, as in several others, has intricate stencils painted by those Minnesota craftsmen so long ago. In 2002, as Robert and Barbara continued refurbishing the home where needed, they zeroed in on the living room ceiling, which had experienced water damage.

They asked a Brookings man to come out of retirement to help re-do those intricate, original ceiling stencil designs his immigrant father and uncle recreated over fifty years ago.

Daryl Petersen, 70, was just out of high school and serving as an apprentice for his father, Valde Petersen, and his uncle Carl, when he watched and learned as they painted the stylish light blue and brown stencils on the living room ceiling.

Apparently, the plastered living room ceiling was damaged in the late 1940s. That's when the Petersen brothers of Brookings were hired to repair and repaint the ceiling and then re-create the original stenciled designs with large corner displays and room-length, colorful border lines applied when the home was being built.

Fifty years later, after more ceiling plaster damage in the room, Daryl returned to work with contractor Mike Johnson of Brookings to restore the ceiling. Johnson said he was fortunate that Petersen was available and willing to apply the stenciling expertise learned from his father.

Petersen used the same straight-edged wooden guides and rulers made from strong Denmark hardwoods that his father had crafted when he was a young apprentice learning the painting and stencil trade in Denmark at the turn of the last century.

"See how straight it is," he said, sighting down the edge of the long wooden brush guide with one edge slightly beveled to prevent the blotting of paint. "It hasn't warped a bit and it must be one hundred years old if not older. Feel how heavy it is."

Petersen also used the knives, special brushes, and other tools that his father either brought with him from Copenhagen when he came to Brookings in 1911, or that he acquired here and used during the years he and his brother were painting contractors in Brookings.

"The stenciling project has extra significance for us because we were able to utilize Mr. Petersen's expertise learned from his father and uncle, who worked on the home for a previous generation," Fishback said. "It's interesting that he's using many of the tools that his father used when he re-did the same ceiling stencils over fifty years ago."

Daryl Petersen prepares to apply paint to the stencil taped to the ceiling above him. *Chuck Cecil Photo*

After the Fishbacks and Johnson sought out Petersen's help in the repair and restoration of the ceiling, a search was conducted to find the original stencils, but to no avail. Petersen said he went through dozens of old stencils in his late father's workshop but couldn't find the living room stencil designs. He also thought he might locate the right formula for the light blue and brown paint mixtures his father had used to replicate the original colors. "Sometimes they wrote them out on the edge of the stencil," he said.

"I was pretty sure Dad had saved the stencils he'd used on this ceiling," Petersen said. "He saved lots of stencils.

We found the stencil for designs in some of the other rooms, but not the ones for this room."

So Petersen and Johnson started the job from scratch. First, Johnson repaired the damaged plaster. Then, before painting over the ceiling and the undamaged designs that Petersen's father and uncle had painted, Petersen carefully traced over the designs on thin paper.

He also measured the location of each pattern on the ceiling and noted its color scheme. Then, he experimented until the mixtures of paints were matched exactly to the colors his father and the earlier painters had used. Petersen then retraced the design onto the thicker stencil paper and meticulously cut out the patterns.

Elegant door knobs grace wide, solid wood doors. *Chuck Cecil Photo*

"The largest and most complicated designs are in each corner of the room," he said. He said he's enjoying following in his father's brush strokes.

The beautiful dining room is oval shaped. There is curved glass in the floor to ceiling windows looking out onto a covered, screened porch. *Chuck Cecil Photo*

The living room features a massive fireplace which still has its original, 101-year-old finish. The fireplace is one of three in the house. *Chuck Cecil Photo*

"Working here has brought back a lot of memories of my father and uncle, and of the days when as a young man I helped them work in these very rooms," he said.

More stencils are on the ceiling just off the living room in the unique, oval-shaped dining room trimmed in cherry woodwork. The stencils there are lined with an oval of light bulbs, which mirror the shape of the old dining room table below. Floor to ceiling bay windows off this room are of curved glass and look out onto a curved, screened porch. A kitchen, with space in the wall for a long-ago discarded double-wide ice box, and book-lined library, are also located on the first floor.

A still-functional speaking tube connects the kitchen to the upstairs master bedroom. Near the kitchen is a rope-operated pulley elevator, which was used in the early days when train travel was the mode. The elevator carried the heavy trunks brought by relatives and visitors who traveled to Brookings.

A massive stairway leads to the second floor.

Van Fishback, who is now president of the bank and lives with his family in the home, recalls as a youngster using the stairway banister as a slide. The metal buttons on his trousers left indisputable evidence of his traveling transgressions. "And boy, did I suffer the consequences," he joked.

Among rooms on the second floor is the master bedroom, which features a classical fireplace. The brass speaking tube in this room was often too much of a temptation for the Fishback children, who would crowd around it to listen to their parents' conversations in the kitchen below as they washed the evening meal's dishes.

The third floor features a billiard room with the original billiard table still in use, although often covered now with a ping-pong table top. It is still used as a popular playroom by the grandchildren.

At one time, a large water tank was tucked away behind chimneys and protruding walls on the third floor to provide water to taps throughout the home. That room later became known among family members as "the box room," recalled Van.

An 100-year-old speaking tube in the master bedroom is connected to a similar device in the kitchen so that breakfast orders could be called down. *Chuck Cecil Photo*

Hidden away, it was where empty boxes, paper items, and books and magazines that might be used later were stored. Because accessibility to the room is not easy, it is where the Fishback children "hid out" for a secluded afternoon of games or reading, Van remembered.

An old white barn is still there behind the home. At one time, it held the family's cows, horses, a few sheep, and chickens. Still in the barn are three old carriages and a horse-drawn sleigh.

Throughout the twentieth century and in the twenty-first century, the generations of Fishbacks who have lived in the home have attempted to preserve its original design when repainting or papering was required.

It is truly a work of art, and Van and Barbara Fishback have every intention of maintaining it so that future generations will know the history of those who have called it home.